THE
FAITH IS
STILL THERE

THE
FAITH IS
STILL THERE

DAVID H.C. READ

Abingdon

Nashville

THE FAITH IS STILL THERE

Copyright © 1981 by Abingdon

Library of Congress Cataloging in Publication Data
READ, DAVID HAXTON CARSWELL.
The faith is still there.
1. Apologetics—20th century. 2. United States—Reli-
gion—1960- I. Title.
BT1102.R386   239   80-21395

ISBN 0-687-12650-9

Scripture quotations unless otherwise noted are from the Revised Standard
Version of the Bible, copyrighted 1946, 1952, © 1971 and 1973 by the Division
of Christian Education, National Council of Churches, and are used by
permission.

MANUFACTURED BY THE PARTHENON PRESS AT
NASHVILLE, TENNESSEE, UNITED STATES OF AMERICA

TO JOHN WEAVER
Organist, Choir-Director,
Elder, and Companion in
the faith.

Contents

PREFACE

This book is written from the conviction that the historic Christian faith is not only still alive in the 1980s but offers the strongest sustenance for the mind and spirit in an age of confusion.

By the "historic faith" I mean the gospel as attested in the Scriptures, articulated in the creeds of the early Church, reaffirmed by the Reformers, and kept alive in the worship of the denominations that belong to the mainstream of the Christian tradition. I do not mean the kind of narrow orthodoxy that refuses to think or the literalism that is deaf to the poetry of the faith or any kind of ecclesiastical imperialism.

At a time when the hysterical wing of American religion is so much in evidence, it needs to be demonstrated that the alternative is not a barren skepticism or a secularized version of the faith, but adherence to the catholic tradition under the reforming Spirit of God.

The historic faith is biblical without being obscurantist, rational without being rationalist, supernatural without being unnatural, personal without being individualist, socially active without being secularist, mystical without being escapist, confident without being arrogant, and exciting enough to blow the mind but not to destroy it.

What follows is addressed to that great company who still, with greater or less conviction, adhere to churches where the historic gospel is proclaimed in Word and Sacrament, the Trinity is worshiped, faith nurtured, and the healing ministry of Christ practised and supported at home and abroad. When there is so much confusion of terms— with "born-again," "evangelical," "Bible-believing," and other catchwords being thrown around to describe a certain type of Christian—it is good to be reminded of the mainstream of Christian tradition which, representing the one, catholic, apostolic Church, constantly reforming, includes all genuine believers in Christ as Savior and Lord.

But it is also addressed to those whom, in another generation, Schleiermacher described as the "cultured despisers" of the Christian faith. When the reigning philosophy of secular humanism begins to be threatened by the brutal facts of modern life and by the evidence of the enduring power of religion in the human soul, many will be looking for a basis for living that is less circumscribed and narrow-minded, more responsive to the element of mystery in our experience. It may be that the historic faith will appear again to offer more satisfaction to the mind and spirit than any rival philosophy. It is my hope that this book will stimulate some to question their rejection of a faith they may never have explored, and to find their way home to the Church of Jesus Christ, the Eternal Contemporary.

I am grateful to theologians and artists of all sorts who have expressed the historic faith in our day with loyalty and imagination, to friends whose lives demonstrate it, and to a congregation whose vitality and encouragement confirm my faith. For the skill, humor, and devotion of my secretary, Carolyn Mathis, I remain truly thankful.

"Some cried one thing, and some another: for the assembly was confused; and the more part knew not wherefore they were come together." (Acts 19:32)

1. THE UPROAR OF AMERICAN RELIGION

You have, of course, to be tuned in to hear it. It is quite possible to go about your business, talk to your friends, read a few books and magazines, choose your TV programs, and raise a family without ever being much disturbed by the noises of religion. On the whole the media are not reflecting much genuine religious activity in this country. The newspapers report an occasional horror or scandal that has religious overtones. Some weekly magazines have a lively and informative religious section. Television and radio are invaded by religious spectaculars and dynamic personalities. But few could guess that religion is such a power in modern America from its treatment in the literary world, on the airwaves, or in the popular press. (Lists of bestsellers avoid mention of religious books. "The National Radio Pulpit" is presented to radio-listeners in New York at 1:05 A.M. "Letters to the Editor" screen out any serious religious discussion.)

Yet the startling fact is that the United States is unique among the nations of the Western world in the vitality and upsurge of its religious life. In a recent Gallup poll,

India was the only nation with a higher percentage of its population declaring that their religious beliefs were "very important" to them. We would expect the situation here to be different from that in communist-controlled countries where religion is under open attack or in the lands of the East where Christianity has always been a minority faith. What is new is the surprising difference between the state of religion in the United States and the prevailing trend in other nations of the traditionally Christian West.

Any traveler to Europe in recent years must have noticed the decline in the influence and support of the churches whose ancient shrines are still such an attraction to the tourist. The secularization of Europe has proceeded rapidly in the last thirty years or so. It might almost be said to have reached the stage when moral bankruptcy may compel a fateful decision. Will the receivers be some form of communism or facism— or a revitalization of the faith that inspired the civilization of the West? Those who hope that the last possibility will prevail, must face the fact that religion has now been shunted to the sidelines in most European countries—even those which, like England, Scotland, Germany, Italy, and the Scandinavian nations, still retain some form of Christian establishment. The voice of the Church is now a whisper in lands where once governments were in awe of the sounds emanating from the Vatican, Lambeth, or the Nonconformist conscience. Church attendance has shrunk dramatically; new universities and schools tend to ignore religion; seminaries become more and more politicized; religion appears in books, movies, and television more often as a subject for satire than as an inspiring force. I am told that there are now more Muslims than Methodists in England, and it is probable that, proportionately, there are more atheists in Sweden than in Russia.

Yet in the United States religion is booming. It is by no means the same boom we experienced in the fifties. At that time the traditional churches were growing, and every suburb in America saw new spires pointing to heaven and commodius buildings springing up devoted to Christian education and recreation. The present boom is bypassing the religious establishments and expressing itself in a resurgence of "old-time religion," a growth in the more conservative churches, the appeal of relatively new religious groups such as the Mormons, Jehovah's Witnesses, Seventh-Day Adventists, Scientologists, and the Unification Church of Reverend Moon. Television has spawned an extraordinary number of religious programs associated with a variety of charismatic figures. There are more than thirteen hundred radio and thirty-six television stations in the country that are almost wholly given over to religious broadcasting, and the networks carry numerous evangelistic programs that are paid for by the generous support of the faithful. Religious broadcasting today, in fact, is big business running into billions of dollars.

At the same time there has been a proliferation of movements offering ways of life, techniques of meditation, and assurances of salvation based on the teachings of gurus, ancient and modern. Young people, in particular, are said to be attracted to the kind of mysticism they have failed to find in churches that have been too busy adapting themselves to the so-called "age of scientific rationalism" (that has failed to show up). The adherents of the more exotic cults are perhaps more conspicuous than they are representative of a large percentage of our youth, but they are symptomatic of the search for the transcendent by those who are tired of the rat-race of a materialistic and secular society.

What must puzzle a European visitor is the role that religion plays in public affairs in America. Few countries have more explicitly rejected any form of official religious establishment. "Congress shall make no law respecting an establishment of religion" says the First Amendment to the Constitution. Yet most Europeans observe, to their astonishment, that religious exercises and religious personalities have a much more prominent place here than in almost any country of the old world—even those where a particular Christian church is established and recognized as the "national religion." They find prayers being offered, not only at presidential inaugurations and the opening of every session of Congress, but at ceremonies and public luncheons and dinners of every description. (It also would be a fair guess that the habit of saying "grace" at meals is far more common in America than in any other country of the West.) The observer would also note that politicians here are concerned about the votes of Roman Catholics, Jews, and recently—to the surprise and bewilderment of the press— Evangelicals. Chaplains in the armed forces and in prisons are at last as prominent as in any country with a religious establishment. None of these things could be described as relics of a former piety. All the evidence indicates that this is now a much more religious country than it was when it was founded. It was comparatively recently that In God We Trust appeared on our coins, and Under God was inserted into the pledge of allegiance.

None of this has happened without some uproar from those dedicated to interpreting the First Amendment as raising a wall of separation between church and state. Thus prayers in public schools have been ruled unconstitutional, and controversy surrounds public celebrations of festivals like Christmas and Easter outside the churches. But these very controversies go to show how seriously such questions are regarded by the average American. It would be difficult to imagine any uproar in England or in Scandinavia about the appearance of a member of the clergy on official occasions, or the offering of prayers in public school, or the singing of carols on a village square—not because of any religious fervor but because no one would think it mattered much either way.

What lies behind this intensity of religious feeling in the United States? Let this immigrant (imported Scotch, vintage twenty-five years) hazard a few guesses.

(1) The mere fact that the United States represents an accumulation of immigrants and the descendants of immigrants has marked the country with a sense of vitality and enterprise in every national activity. Even if the exuberance and optimism of previous generations has been moderated by recent events, there is still a unique fund of energy and openness to new ideas lurking in the American soul. And historically this spirit has been linked with a strong religious factor motivating successive immigrations. In the early days Congregationalists, Presbyterians, Roman Catholics, and Anglicans came to these shores seeking religious freedom (a freedom they were not always willing to grant one another!). And in recent years, Jews, Hungarians, Baltic peoples, Cubans, and many others have immigrated seeking freedom to exercise their faith. All this keeps religion in the forefront of American thinking and insures a liveliness of religious practice and debate. It might even be said that the very diversity of religious belief has contributed to the strength of religion by the deep-rooted American principle that competition is good for business.

(2) From the beginning the frontier spirit has had strong religious implications. Those who pushed out into the wilderness with chiefly material gain in view were soon followed by Methodists and Baptists eager to claim each new community for the gospel of Christ, and the lands of the west soon became fertile breeding grounds for new sects with special appeal to those who had lost their religious roots. The spirit of adventure infected the religious scene in a way seldom to be found in the Old World. And this has not died away. It is truly American to view the exploration of

outer space in the light of the biblical injunction to have dominion over the works of creation, and other nations listened with surprise to one of the first astronauts quoting Genesis as he orbited the moon.

(3) The arrival in this country of so many varied religious traditions and the capacity of Americans for inventing new religions has given rise to what is now called the phenomenon of pluralism. What this means in practice is that more than most other people today Americans inevitably encounter at close quarters people with very different beliefs from their own. Increased mobility has insured that few pockets remain where one particular religion is totally dominant. This could have led to a spirit of indifference to all religions, and indeed there are some who draw the conclusion that with so many competing voices claiming to speak for God, it is best to be skeptical about them all. But generally the opposite has happened. Not only have Jews, Roman Catholics, and Protestants stimulated one another to take their own faiths more seriously, but the constant emergence of evangelists, from the most orthodox to the most outrageous, has kept religion high on the conversational totem pole.

(4) This leads me to remark on a distinctive feature of American opinion—its tolerance of almost any belief or behavior that bears a religious label. Apart from those who are flamingly convinced of the total truth and exclusive right to salvation of their own brand of religion, the great majority of Americans are prepared to accept uncritically whatever is offered in God's name. Religions of all kinds proliferate in this country because it is considered not only unkind but intolerant to question what is being said or done in the name of God. The questionable principle, "all religions are good," is deeply ingrained in the American soul, and it took the Guyana horror of 1978, when hundreds of cultists were induced to commit suicide at the behest of their leader, to

awaken many to the thought that some religions may be bad—as the Bible would say, demonic.

(5) Behind these factors contributing to the strength of religion in modern America there lies, I believe, an ineradicable strain of genuine piety. In theological circles it is fashionable to mock at what is called public religion—the kind of emotion that unites Americans on Thanksgiving Day or on any occasion of national stress, such as the holding of the hostages in Iran. It is easy to caricature such emotions as an attempt to clothe nationalist emotions with the trappings of religion. Foreigners like to portray Americans as using religion to exalt "God's own country" and as disguising their material ambitions with talk about their "manifest destiny" under God. No one could claim that the United States has been exempt from the hyprocrisy and arrogance that have stained the record of every powerful nation the world has ever seen, but there is more than one way of singing "My country, 'tis of thee." I believe there is an intense strain of genuine piety in America that humbly acknowledges the God "from whom all blessings flow," and to a greater extent than most nations, seeks the guidance and wisdom that come from beyond all human resources and, to put it simply, still believes in prayer.

These, and many other, factors have contributed to both the vitality and the confusion of contemporary American religion. It ought to be added that United States citizens have, since World War II, been much more sensitive to the threat of communism than other Western nations, and the atheism of the Marxist philosophy looms larger in popular thinking. Godless communism is a slogan certain to arouse emotions in any political campaign. Hence for some decades religion has, genuinely or cynically, been regarded as a valuable ally in the ideological struggle. At its best this linking of religion and international politics has led to a new awareness that theology is not an antiquated academic exercise but lies at the root of the great questions that agitate the human race. There is some understanding that behind political issues lie ethical ones, and behind the ethical there must always be the question of a God from whom our values are derived. At its worst this tie-up of religion and politics produces an alarming blend of extreme fundamentalist religion and extreme rightwing politics—the same heady mixture we deplore in the militant Islam of an Ayatollah Khomeini.

What has puzzled and disturbed many observers of the current religious scene in this country is that in the uproar of religion, the softest voices seem to come from the churches of the historic denominations. The traditional Reformed churches (Presbyterian, Methodist, Congregational), the Anglican communion, the Roman Catholic, and the Orthodox, have not been experiencing any noticeable resurgence of religious enthusiasm or producing charismatic figures to capture national attention. A favorite topic for observers of the religious scene has been the decline in membership and attendance in the more liberal mainline churches as contrasted with the growth of the more conservative and fundamentalist bodies. It is very evident that the social and cultural pressures that led to the strength and expansion of the historic denominations just after World War II are no longer operative and that standard-brand worship and church activity have lost what attraction they had for the average citizen.

There are some quick and tempting answers to the phenomenon of declining mainline churches and expanding conservative ones. In a time of great insecurity and confusion most people like to get their religion straight, with no if's or but's. They want dogmatic reassurance and prefer not to be bothered by questions of theological credibility, or of how to relate the faith to contemporary social and political issues. It is always easier, too, for a local church to thrive if it concentrates on one dogmatic interpretation of the faith and appeals to one social group. A church that tries to be truly catholic in its proclamation and application of the gospel, and in its appeal to every kind of person, is much less likely to find an enthusiastic popular response. Since Americans are more apt to be impressed by numbers than are other observers of the religious scene, there is a temptation to fall back on the elitist argument that the mainline churches need not worry. After all there is always a bigger audience for rock music than for Beethoven, and Johnny Carson draws higher TV ratings than Shakespeare.

Those of us who are concerned about the future of the historic churches would be foolish to console ourselves with this kind of reflection. We are right not to be sandbagged by the numbers game, but we have no justification whatever for smugly assuming that when the uproar has died down millions of sensible people will come flocking back to the traditional denominations. Statistics of membership and attendance may not be the main criteria for assessing the true strength of a denomination, but we should remember that it is recorded in the book of Acts that, after the apostolic faith had winged its way across the Graeco-Roman world, "day by day, the congregations grew stronger in faith and increased in numbers." If the churches today that claim continuity with that apostolic faith are not making an impact comparable to that of more recent sects and less "catholic" churches, the answer lies deeper than any surface judgment about popular appeal, and we must not succumb to complacent assurance that we are offering the fullness of the gospel and the ubiquity of its challenge. We have some hard thinking to do. We have some Bible study to do. And we have some praying to do.

The historic denominations could be so called because they have preserved in theology and their liturgies the beliefs and practices that have marked the Christian community since New Testament times. Unlike many of the sects, they do not focus upon some unique revelation given to a dynamic character of the nineteenth or twentieth century. Even those marked by the name of a reformer, like Luther or Wesley, do not think of their church as founded by, or resting upon, such an authority. In one way or another the historic denominations claim continuity with the Church of the apostles. The Roman Catholic, the Orthodox, and the Anglican communions emphasize this by a specific doctrine of apostolic succession. Protestants of the Reformed, Lutheran, and Methodist traditions have also claimed this heritage and are prepared to affirm, with varying degrees of enthusiasm: "I believe in one, Holy, Catholic, and Apostolic Church." In the theological polemics and liturgical upheaval of the Reformation this note of continuity was never lost by the major Protestant bodies. Luther, Calvin, and Knox, throughout the turmoil of the period, believed themselves to be struggling, not to establish a new religion, but for the apostolic gospel and for a form of worship and style of church government that more nearly reflected what they found in the New Testament. The continuity was expressed, not only in their insistence of the centrality of Holy Scripture, but by their retention of the Apostles' and Nicene creeds, their emphasis on the sacraments of Baptism and Holy Communion, and their use of the hymns and collects of the early church.

It is precisely this sense of continuity, this historic ingredient of the faith, that has been muted in so many of the mainline churches in recent years. Laboring under the curse of so-called relevance, the historic denominations have been behaving as though we had no heritage of faith and worship to proclaim and enjoy but rather the task of making an adjustment to the spirit of the age. (Dean Inge used to say that whoever marries the spirit of the age is doomed soon to become a widower—and there are many widower-signs around us in the eighties). The sixties were, by and large, a period of amnesia when churches tended to act as though they had no history. All that mattered was adjusting to a society that was restless and iconoclastic, to a culture that was rootless and kaleidoscopic, and to a popular philosophy that was supposed to be totally secular in its presuppositions. So the churches broke out in a rash of indiscriminate activism, liturgical experimentation, and a radical repudiation of traditional beliefs, culminating in the theological suicide known as the Death of God.

A sudden swing of the pendulum in the seventies meant a retreat from this mood of radical readjustment, this worship at the shrine of relevance. The Now-generation became the Me-generation. The churches turned inward and became immersed either in their internal affairs (the next blessed word was "restructuring") or in the rediscovery of a lost spirituality. But there was little sign of a true recovery of our heritage. Amnesia was not succeeded by an awakening to the latent power of the historic faith but by the nostalgia that is the illegitimate daughter of a sense of history. When members of mainline churches began demanding a return to the "faith of our fathers," the fathers they had in mind were not Paul, Augustine, Aquinas, Luther, and Calvin, but Moody and Sankey and other stalwarts of turn-of-the-century religion.

All such judgments are, of course, sweeping and often unfair. There was a genuine response to the Spirit in much of the activism of the sixties and the search for spirituality in the seventies. The argument of this book is not for a sterile traditionalism that sits smugly on the conventional creeds, scorning and denouncing every attempt to relate them to what is indeed a revolutionary world, a world that has changed more in the last fifty years than in the previous five hundred. Part of the historic faith is a belief in the Holy Spirit, "the Lord and Giver of life," and that Spirit is the contemporizer of Christian faith and life. What we should be seeking is not a return to some idealized church of our nostalgic dreams, but a moving forward in the confidence that the gospel of Christ, who is the same yesterday, today, and tomorrow, can be understood and accepted and realized afresh with each new challenge of the accelerating history of the human race; and that, in the words of John Robinson, "God hath yet more light to break forth from his Holy Word" (by a happy slip of the typewriter I found I had written "loving forward," and was tempted to let it stand).

If this great mass of Christians who are neither skeptics nor fanatics is to make an impact on modern society proportionate to its numbers, we need to recover our nerve, rediscover our roots, and produce a generation of instructed and dedicated believers whose religion is not a private predilection ("attend the church of your choice") but the mainspring of their lives as citizens of a bewildering, dangerous, and yet entrancing, world. We will need theological guts—more than can be supplied by an occasional twenty-minute sermon. One of the encouraging signs today is the increasing demand for biblical instruction and a new study of the creeds and confessions of the Church. We will need men and women who are equipped to represent the faith in the media, literature, and the arts, not as crude propagandists, but as believers in the Tale that has been the inspiration of our cultural heritage.

We will need a new piety. It may be too late to resurrect that word (Who wants to be known as "pious"?), but the qualities of reverence, humility, trust, and courage that it originally implied can revolutionize the mainline churches. Both clergy and laity seem to be groping for new ways of prayer and devotion, and we cannot expect to be satisfied with the patterns of other ages. Fortunately, there are writers better equipped than this one to stimulate our search for that communion with God without which all that is discussed in these pages is as a tinkling cymbal. The most helpful sign of all in the current uproad of American religion is the emergence of men and women—neither skeptic nor fanatic—who are unostentatiously both talking and listening to God.

2. *"WITH ALL THY MIND"*
ROOM FOR A REASONED RELIGION

Let me try to imagine how an intelligent student, with little or no affiliation to a church or synagogue, emerging from college in the 1980s, would regard the religious scene in this country. I think it would be obvious that, even if few professors or lecturers seemed to have noticed it, religion is still a powerful force in American society. If our student's experience has been confined to a study of the modern novel or the movies, a perusal of the literary or political views, the chatter of the seminar, and the fervent nonattendance of his colleagues at church or chapel, there might well be a kind of cultural shock on entering what commencement speakers are apt to call the mainstream of American life. For religion would suddenly appear as a force to be reckoned with for good or ill.

It would strike her (or him) that the blithe assumption of academia, that religion is a spent intellectual force, a subject of interest only to the historian, the anthropologist, the nostalgic, or the nut, is by no means verified by the facts of modern American life. Not only is an extraordinarily large proportion of the population affiliated with a church or synagogue, but religion keeps cropping up in the debates that rage around topics like abortion, disarmament, foreign aid, censorship, education, and human rights. If a new translation of the New Testament appears and, in a few years, some sixty million copies are sold, our student may conclude that someone is reading it. Churches may not appear to be as thriving as they were in the fifties, but even as they thrash around debating internal questions of structure and polity (and occasionally theology) a surprising number of people seem to care. Then there is the proliferation of religious movements, with little or no connection with the accepted denominations, popularly called cults. There must be few families who have escaped having a child, a grandmother, an uncle, or at least a distant cousin, swept into enthusiastic affiliation with some cult. How ever nonsensical the beliefs they have embraced seem to the rest of the family, no one can deny the immense power of the religious passions that are unleashed.

A curious dichotomy faces our student as she observes the current religious scene. On the one hand, in cultural and academic circles and among the leaders of opinion as expressed in the dominant media of our day, religion is either ignored or, in its more sensational manifestations, treated as a kind of mythological disease. The reigning philosophy is a tolerant and agnostic humanism that shudders at the thought of actually embracing any religious doctrine as the truth. On the other hand, we find a nation where 94 percent of the population professes to believe in God, and where 36 percent confesses that their religious beliefs are very important. This dichotomy leads to some curious adjustments when our student, trained in an atmosphere of religious skepticism, makes contact with the believing world in the arena of politics, medicine, or law. Faced with the power of religion, one trained in skepticism must either reexamine the whole question or cynically decide how to manipulate the religious convictions of the average citizen. I am reminded of Edward Gibbon's classic description of the state of religion in the Roman Empire. "The various modes of worship, which prevailed in the Roman world, were all considered by the people as equally true, by the philosopher, as equally false; and by the magistrate as equally useful."

What is happening now is, in my opinion, a subtle attempt to present the intelligent citizen with a painfully limited choice. One must either adopt a genial, skeptical humanist philosophy, remaining, in the fold of some respectable denomination but not taking its doctrines too seriously; or one can take a deep breath, close one's eyes, and plunge into the embrace of a cult that offers the security of absolute truth about this world and the next at the modest price of a total suspension of all your critical faculties. At the time of Alexandr Solzhenitsyn's controversial Harvard speech the *New York Times* spelled out this false dilemma with the comment: "At bottom it is the argument between the religious enthusiasts, sure of their relationship to the divine will, and the man of the Enlightenment, trusting in the rationality of humankind." Solzhenitsyn thus became the symbol of religious fanaticism, and his expression of the historic Christian faith was written off in the title of the article as "Solzhenitsyn's Obsession."

Thus the myth is being propagated that there is no other alternative to a blind, obscurantist, fanatical adherence to some religion that demands a total sacrifice of not only the soul, but the body and the mind as well, than a secular humanism that remains skeptical about any religious claims whatever. The thoughtful citizen, whether affiliated or not with a church or synagogue, is thus pushed into a corner. If you don't want to become a fanatic the only way left is religious skepticism based on a philosophy that trusts in what the *Times* called "the rationality of humankind." Before we examine this assessment of the choice before us, let me note that it is being steadily propagated by what can only be called the "secularist establishment" of our day. It is now dawning on many of us that when the dogma of the separation of church and state is pushed to its extreme, we end up with an educational system, a popular philosophy, and a network of national media instilling the dogmas of secular humanism. There is no such thing as a philosophic vacuum, or religious neutralist. If we are not promoting one view of life, we are promoting another. Agnosticism is not a neutral gear into which we can shift while the car goes merrily on. It is one of the gears we can choose, and there are consequences to be reckoned with. One of these consequences is the spread of the notion that religion is a side issue in modern society, a decoration some like to add to life's daily cake, a hobby to be pursued by those who have a taste for it, or a sociological phenomenon with occasional sensational entertainment value.

One can make this diagnosis of the status of religion only if one ignores the enduring presence in our society of a body of belief recognizable as continuous with the affirmations of the Christian faith in every century and in every land. The Roman Catholic, Orthodox, and major Protestant churches (representing some 120 million people in this country) officially adhere to a body of beliefs symbolized by the Apostles' and Nicene creeds. Even allowing for the fact that among Protestants and, to some extent, among Roman Catholics there is debate and uncertainty about the interpretation of these creeds, with some churches not using them at all, there is a powerful consensus of belief in the Triune God. The historic confession of faith in God the Father Almighty, in Jesus Christ as his only Son our Lord, and in the Holy Spirit as the Lord and Giver of life, is still there in the written statements of belief and also in the worship, the thinking, and the personal piety of this vast number of believers. Looked at in the light of the ideological struggle in the modern world, where communism, secularism, and various forms of nationalism (not to mention the growing militancy of Islam and the pervasive influence of Buddhism) are competing for the human soul, it is really extraordinary that this affirmation of the enduring Christian convictions is still being made by such a large proportion of the population of the United States. When one considers the truly astonishing and mind-boggling nature of the Christian creed with its central proclamation that in a Jewish teacher, who was executed two thousand years ago by the Romans, the Creator-God revealed himself to the whole human race and offered a way of deliverance and hope, it is some kind of a miracle that this faith is still there. Compared with Christianity, the intellectual demand and appeal of communism, Islam, or Buddhism are relatively simple and credible. It must also be obvious that, compared with the vast gulf yawning between the historic Christian faith and all other convictions and ways of life, the questions of belief and practice separating the denominations are comparatively trivial.

If, then, this massive testimony to the historic Christian faith is present in our culture, why is it so often suppressed in the current debate about religion? Why is it being assumed in many quarters that the choice before us is between skepticism and fanaticism? Why does the intellectual get away with his assumption that the only living religion in our society is to be found among those devoid of any critical judgment, those whose minds have been captivated by some charismatic figure or who have blindly accepted the tenets of some aggressive sect? Why does the average citizen who is not connected with a church or synagogue get the impression that the only way to be religious today is to succumb to the hysteria of the cults or deliver one's mind and soul to the loudest and most arrogant voices on radio or television?

One obvious answer lies in the nature and power of the media. Popular journalism, printed or electronic, is naturally attracted to the extreme and the bizarre. If "dog bites man" is not news, neither is the fact that hundreds of thousands of churches are devoted week in and week out to propagating the historic Christian faith. But sensational pronouncements about an immediate return of Christ, the appearance of instant messiahs, and the denunciation of orthodox churches as synagogues of Satan, or the apparent discovery by some far-out theologians that God is dead (remember?)—all this falls into the man-bites-dog category. The power of the media is such that when the airwaves are filled with blandishments of rival authorities appealing chiefly to the emotions of fear and hope, it is not surprising that the thoughtful citizen begins to equate religion with mindless fanaticism. Since broadcast religion has become big business, the good time-slots are dominated by those who know how to make it pay, while more moderate voices are gently shunted to such hours as 6 A.M. on what is known as public affairs time. (I hope this does not sound like the lament of a disgruntled National Radio Pulpit preacher!) I confess that were I just now experiencing an awakened interest in religion, a great deal of what I hear on radio and TV would tend to repel me.

But it would be quite unfair to blame the neglect of orthodox Christianity on the machinations of the media. A more solid reason is the impression given by those of us who remain attached in such large numbers to the inheritance of the Christian past. We have given the impression that we are content to be just that—stolid defenders of a religious status quo, finding neither skepticism nor fanaticism quite respectable, and trusting vaguely that the nation will come to its senses and in the next generation will somehow eventually return to the accepted decencies of the past. The conventional orthodoxy of this great mass of traditional Christianity may indeed indicate that the faith is still there, but it is muted faith, tamed and domesticated, a faith that often seems light-years away from the excitement and sense of expectancy reflected, for instance, in the book of Acts. The mainline churches may preserve the historic creeds, but we often give the impression that they are museum pieces to be venerated like relics in our liturgies rather than the battle-cry of believers in the most dynamic and astonishing gospel ever heard on earth. Few would guess from the way in which millions mumble these ancient words that they are really a bold declaration of a powerful, reasoned, and uncompromising religious conviction to be thrown in the face of the world, the flesh, and the devil.

Now, it may be, we have come to the crux of the matter. Do those who represent the mainstream of Christianity in our society really believe that the historic faith can hold its own in debate with the philosophies and ideologies of the modern world? We no longer live in a world where the average church member is surrounded by a society reflecting the basic Christian convictions. There is no supporting climate of opinion, such as once permeated all "Christendom," one that enabled us to go on our way assured that the Christian tenets in which we had been trained were supported by the great majority of right-thinking people. Not only are academia, the media, and popular opinion almost entirely captivated by a secularist philosophy in which religion is tolerated as a private aberration, but even in the religious field itself, we are exposed to a bewildering pluralism. Never before have the alternatives to orthodox Christianity been so visible in the Western world.

If one wants a religion, the problem is which one to choose—Zen Buddhism, Islam, Hari Krishna, Moon's Unification Church, Christian Science, Mormonism, Spiritism or the Worldwide Church of God? And if the individual opts for a church that holds the historic Christian faith, how can he be sure that it will, in fact, be holding steadily and intelligently to the faith? The rumbles from the theologians that reach the ears of the ordinary church member are not reassuring, and sometimes the church must appear to be undermined from within. I am not talking here about the kind of orthodoxy associated with Fundamentalism, which is at the moment attracting those who are alarmed at this shaking of the foundations, but about the basic Christian affirmations of the Triune God and the classic Christian doctrines of creation, the fall, and of redemption through Jesus Christ. The so-called mainline churches demonstrate such hesitancy and loss of nerve, that our contemporaries may well ask: What do they believe?

What has been lacking, in my opinion, is a willingness to grapple with the content of the historic faith in the light of our new situation. How much of the teaching in our elaborate system of Christian education, how many sermons, are devoted to the basic doctrines of the faith? What knowledge of the Bible is there in our churches beyond a nodding acquaintance with the snippets regularly read at worship? In the avalanche of books dealing with personal life-adjustment, relationships, self-improvement, sex, security, and controversial topics like euthanasia, abortion, and political choices, how many do we find wrestling with the Christian story as set out in the Bible, with the creeds and confessions of the Church? I am not for a moment recommending that we ignore the practical problems confronting us twentieth-century Christians, or despising the pastoral efforts of the Church to minister to the deepest needs of the human soul, but I am protesting that the time has come to reaffirm the central tenets of the faith and obey the commandment to love the Lord our God *with all our minds.*

There is always a pendulum motion in the Church as it faces its task of proclaiming and living the gospel in each generation. If I were to speculate about what has been happening and may, please God, be about to happen, I would say that the sixties were a period when the energies of the churches were concentrated on the practical expression of the faith, or what is popularly known as activism. There was a revolt against conventional piety, against traditional forms of worship, against Christian ethics that denounced adultery, promiscuity, laziness, and street crime but said little about war, exploitation, racial prejudice, and oppression. The theology of this period was derived largely from the Hebrew prophets, whose attack on religious formalism and strident demand for social justice is undoubtedly a part of the faith. At its most extreme, however, this revolutionary phase seemed to many to secularize and politicize the gospel, and many were left wondering why they needed the church to participate in the creation of a better world, and what was left of Christianity if there was no creed worth bothering about, no supernatural dimension, no transcendence in worship—and perhaps even no God.

Then there was a reaction. The seventies, have been a period of return to the spiritual (as some might put it) or a flight from social responsibilities (as others would prefer to say). One way or another, it has been a time of intense concern with the inner life—with prayer, meditation, and what is vaguely known as "spirituality." The churches have been responding to this mood, but one of the striking features of the decade has been the search for spirituality beyond the frontiers of the established churches. It is as if those who hungered after the transcendental, after new experience of prayer, after the mystic way, had concluded that the churches had little to offer, and were immediately attracted by cults and teachers offering something new or, occasionally, something very, very old.

What has been missing in both decades has been a concern for a reasoned faith, a grasp of the gospel that satisfies the mind as well as the heart. Very few voices have been heard pleading for the place of intelligence in the life of faith. As one who was raised in a theological atmosphere that has always stressed the use of the mind—the Calvinist tradition, which for centuries dominated Presbyterianism in Europe and in this country—I confess that I succumbed in part to the denigration of the intellect that characterized both the sixties and the seventies. And I am not sorry that these decades forced me to consider more seriously than before the social implications of the creeds and confessions and the fact that the emotions are as valid as the mind in our response to the gospel. So for a while I shied away from the field of popular apologetics, the attempt to commend the faith in intellectual terms to the contemporary world. Yet the wheel turns, and this book is designed to do just that. I have come to believe that the eighties could be a time when the mainline churches reassert the place of a reasoned faith, and rediscover the true teaching office of the Church.

Again, I would stress that this cannot be done by deploying the energies of the Christian mind in an all-out effort to reestablish every jot and tittle of the creeds of our grandparents. I have no interest in an educated obscurantism. The orthodoxy I am defending is that of the central doctrine of the faith as declared in the creed of the Roman Catholic and Eastern Orthodox churches, and the World Council of Churches. Peter Berger, in a new book, maintains that there is really no such thing as Christian orthodoxy any more, since there is no supporting community of faith when a whole nation officially professed Roman Catholicism, Anglicanism, or Presbyterianism. He says we are now all called to choose—and thus to become heretics (for etymologically "heretic" derives from a word meaning "to make a choice"). "For this notion of heresy to have any meaning at all," he says, "there was presupposed the authority of a religious tradition. . . . The heretic denied this authority, refused to accept the tradition in toto. Instead he picked and chose from the content of the tradition, and from these pickings and choosings constructed his own deviant opinion." Berger suggests that the modern situation forces us all to be heretics insofar as we cannot just blindly accept a given religion, for there aren't any such any more. In this sense, then, I will accept that I am a heretic—but the choice I am forced to make in these pluralistic times is for the historic Christian faith, and I gather that Berger does the same. I welcome his masterly analysis of our situation and his implied plea for the use of our minds as we make this choice. From this you will begin to understand the title of his book *The Heretical Imperative.*

If Christianity today is regarded in many quarters as a negligible force in the battle for the mind, if there are few outstanding philosophers who are professed Christians, if it is popularly assumed that a sermon will be intellectually inferior to the speech of a politician or the writings of a columnist, then one can only conclude that this Christian generation has not lived up to the traditions of the past. To reel off the names of brilliant minds who have molded the thinking of the Western world would be an exercise in Christian name-dropping: Paul, Augustine, Aquinas, Calvin, Luther are only at the tip of the iceberg that has floated through our civilization and shaped the thoughts and destinies of millions. From the beginning Christianity received a rich intellectual heritage with its Jewish swaddling-clothes. It is written of the first followers of Jesus that the authorities "perceived that they were unlearned and ignorant men," (which is a salutary reminder to anyone engaged on an exercise like this that the validity of the faith has nothing to do with one's I.Q.), but each one of them had been instructed at home and in the synagogue school, and was by no means prepared to surrender his duty to defend his beliefs with his reasoning powers. "Be prepared," wrote Peter, "to give a reason for the faith that is in you." The inclusion in the first commandment of the demand to love God "with all thy mind" was no accident. This is demonstrated by the enormous emphasis on education and the training of the intellect from Old Testament times until today, with results that are obvious to all.

When the gospel began to spread to the Gentile world, however, the majority of its converts were often either slaves or people with very limited education, and Christianity therefore might well not have broken through to become a dominant religious force in the Roman Empire. Like many other sects it would simply have disappeared, if there had not been a succession of thinkers to continue the work of Paul in challenging not only the morals but also the philosophies of the time. The Epistle to the Romans is an example of the working of the Christian mind within the Church, and it has never ceased to stimulate the thoughtful as well as instruct the devout. An example of how the apostle attempted to reason for the faith in the presence of the Athenian intelligentsia is preserved in Luke's famous summary of the speech to the eggheads of the Areopagus. From then on the Church, as it has been remarked, was set on a course not only to out-live and out-love, but also to out-think, the pagan world. In tracts and treaties, in public and private debate, the Christians sought to translate what had been a very Jewish-sounding message in terms that made sense to the Graeco-Roman world, and to this day the works of the early fathers represent an intellectual achievement that not even our modern pagans can despise. Within the church the same intellectual fervor was at work hammering out the doctrines later expressed in the creeds of Nicaea and Chalcedon. Then in the fourth century the towering figure of Augustine rose up in Africa, and his literary works not only blazed the way for the Latin Church through the Dark Ages and influenced all subsequent Christian civilization but also have won him the reputation as one of the dozen or so writers that any serious intellectual must know.

The time would fail me, as the writer of the Epistle to the Hebrews used to say, to tell of Abelard, Anselm, Aquinas, Calvin, Luther, Erasmus, and the whole host of brilliant thinkers who not only shaped the thinking of Europe but inspired its greatest art. Since then every century has produced its crop of giants: Pascal, Newton, Kant, Kierkegaard, Schleiermacher, Barth (to mention only a few), who professed the faith and interpreted it, each to his own generation with immense intellectual vigor and conviction. Walter Lippman, writing his *Preface to Morals* in 1929, did full justice to the immense power of what he called "the Christian Tale," in other words, the orthodox doctrines of Creation and the Fall, and of Redemption through the crucified and risen Christ. He simply lamented that there was nothing comparable in the modern world to the massive intellectual power and inspiring influence on art provided by the Christian gospel. And, in the spirit of the twenties, he felt sadly compelled to confess that the acceptance of this Tale was no longer possible for an honest thinker trained in the concepts and thought-forms of an age of science.

That was exactly fifty years ago. I would contend that in the interim much has happened politically, culturally, and scientifically to make many doubt the dogma that no intelligent man or woman could possibly accept the major doctrines of the Christian faith. We are beyond the point when, even in the popular mind, it seemed that only a materialist philosophy made sense and any religious beliefs must be relegated to the realm of superstition and wishful thinking. Materialism as a hypothesis about the nature of the universe is so intellectually bankrupt that, according to some authorities, communist powers have serious problems finding first-class scientists who are orthodox Marxists. One could list a surprising number of intellectuals during these fifty years who have shocked their contemporaries by embracing the Christian faith. A remarkable thing about these conversions is that in nearly every instance the faith accepted was not one of the watered-down versions promulgated by the avant-garde theologians but the historic credo, intellectual thorns and all.

So surely the time has come for a bolder look at what Luke called "the things most surely believed among us," and a less apologetic kind of apologetics. The signs are that there is a growing appetite—and not only among church people—for a reasoned statement of these "things." Hans Kung's *On Being a Christian* is being devoured in unexpected places. C. S. Lewis's scintillating expositions of the faith in both argument and fantasy are now selling in greater quantity than when he was alive. And it is still true that, in spite of the tidal wave of cults and new religions, no rival faith has appeared with a fraction of the intellectual power and cohesion of the Christian gospel. What prevents the resurgence of historic Christianity in our day is a strange combination of fear, misplaced tolerance, and mental laziness.

Fear—because in the prevailing atmosphere of skepticism, agnosticism, and secularist propaganda, many Christians cling to their faith as a precious plant that must not be exposed to the rigors of the intellectual climate. It is to be protected from exposure to thoughts that might wither it. And so we are tempted into a strange double life, in which we believe certain things on our knees or in church but are unable, or unwilling, to articulate them at the club or the cocktail party. To open the windows seems risky. Better keep these delicate convictions in a safe corner. It can be very painful to expose some of our conventional beliefs to the scrutiny of the mind, our own and other peoples'. But the Bible doesn't tell us that belief is easy, and I hope nothing I have said offers a promise that a solid grasp on the central doctrines of the faith can be had by a simple train of argument. It *is* possible to be possessed by a belief that you are not able to defend to your entire intellectual satisfaction. For faith is ultimately *trust* and not a satisfaction of the mind's demands. I am saying that we should be willing to let the light of reason beat upon every conviction and not try to keep it snug in some isolated corner of the soul.

Tolerance is in many ways a hallmark of the American way of life. Few countries are more ready to let a man or woman profess and practice any conceivable kind of religion, and it is regarded as un-American ever to publicly attack someone else's cherished beliefs. In our age of pluralism this has led to a lessening of the prejudices and antagonisms that have poisoned society in the past. But there is also misplaced tolerance, expansion of this willingness to live and let live until it appears there is really no truth to be discovered, that one opinion is as good as another. At that point religion is nothing more than a matter of taste. Our desire to appear tolerant has led to a muffling of open debate about religious convictions. It is considered improper to acquire such strong convictions about religion that one is led to pronounce conflicting doctrines wrong. This is not tolerance. It is a denial of the critical faculties God has given us. Do we really think it doesn't matter if our neighbor is swept up in a movement that may end in mass-suicide?

This easy tolerance is closely linked with the factor I have dared to call mental laziness. The easy excuses: "There's truth in all religions," or "Why worry about a cult or religion so long as it makes its members happy," or "I don't want to become a fanatic," are used to relieve ourselves from the rigors of thinking through our faith. The result is that the mainline churches are full of people who have never attempted to synchronize their religious thinking with the development of their thought in other categories. Their knowledge of science, of literature, of history, of art, of politics has developed over the years, but often their religious understanding seems to have ground to a stop somewhere around age ten or twelve. No wonder they are afraid to drag some of these ideas out into the daylight of their adult understanding. All of us, clergy and laity, need to devote more time and energy to this aspect of our Christian witness. That is why I am flogging my own brain this Lent to review the "things most surely believed among us," and why I am inviting you to this demanding adventure of the mind.

3. *"MOST SURELY BELIEVED"*
THE CASE FOR THE CREEDS

In this chapter I want to address myself to anyone who agrees that the time has come for the so-called mainline churches to reaffirm their common faith, to exercise the mind again in a study of basic Christian doctrines, and to confront a pluralistic and cult-ridden society with a clear and compelling alternative to skepticism on the one hand and fanaticism on the other. That question has to do with the believability for the average church member of the historic creeds and confessions of the Church. It is all very well to say that there is this huge bloc of Christians, comprising probably more than half the population of this country, who belong to churches that profess the Apostles' Creed in their liturgies or manuals of belief, but does that warrant the assertion (complete with exclamation-mark) that "The Faith Is Still There"?

Would any neutral observer watching a typical congregation struggling to its feet on a Sunday morning to mumble "I believe in God, the Father Almighty" really get the impression that here is a group of believers joyfully voicing the convictions that unite them and hurling defiance at the world, the flesh, and the devil? If an enthusiastic pastor leading his flock in worship were to make the suggestion that at this point all should raise their arms to heaven and shout aloud "the things which are most surely believed among us," in most cases the response would be somewhat disappointing. Decorum apart, not many would be willing to shout more than the first few lines, while most would rather have their hands behind their backs, perhaps with their fingers crossed at certain specific statements. If this is not a caricature we have to ask what is wrong—and then to admit that for a great percentage of this body of believers the ancient creeds evoke at best a tepid acquiesence in a liturgical act that reeks comfortably of a tradition they do not want to lose and, at worst, a very uncomfortable feeling of hypocrisy in being asked to repeat some things they neither understand nor really believe.

The clergy can go on explaining year after year that (a) repeating the creed is not like signing your name to a legal affidavit, but simply a declaration of beliefs that have been held for centuries in the Christian church; (b) that no one is being forced to say aloud those particular affirmations that may be bothersome; and (c) that it is curious that people should make a fuss over repeating some items in the creed when they never raise a squeal about being asked to sing hymns that contain statements that are far more hair-raising (or obscure). Somehow the wording of the creeds causes difficulties, for men and women raised in a totally different world from that of the fourth century, as the verbal expression of the Christianity in which they want to believe. They are also aware, from the occasional tidbits that are leaked from the theological schools or from high-ranking church officials, that modern Christian scholars are often propounding views that are hard to square with the plain man's understanding of the contents of the creed.

This sort of difficulty with the creeds is nothing new. From at least the beginning of this century there have been growls from the laity about being asked to profess such things as the Virgin Birth, the return of Christ to judge the quick and the dead, and the resurrection of the body. And there has been sniping from the theologians at the antiquated cosmology on which the creeds seem to be based—with expressions like "came down from heaven" and "descended into hell," not to mention the ancient Greek philosophy implied in phrases like "being of one substance with the Father, begotten not made." It is doubtful, however, if these considerations form the real obstacle to an acceptance of the creeds today. There is a much greater acceptance of the fact that religion has a right to its own language, even if some of it dates from a pre-Copernican understanding of the universe. Few people seem to be as worried as some theologians have been about the use of spatial imagery like "up" and "down" to express the Christian message. We are so compassed about with the jargon of modern bureaucracy, sociology, and psychiatry that sometimes the language of the creeds, or of the King James' Bible, is greeted with a sigh of relief. We are also by this time more than tired of hearing about the modern, scientifically trained mind that cannot accept anything that smacks of the supernatural. The skeptical generation predicted by some Christian apologists of the thirties and forties, which was supposed to be impervious to any assertions of religion that seemed to contradict the evidence of the senses or the laws of physics, failed to show up. We are now living through one of the most believing, not to say superstitious, periods in modern history. In a world of horoscopes, crystal-gazers, UFOs, extra-sensory perception, and science-fiction, when cults with the wildest irrational claims find ready takers, it is not surprising that not so many are losing sleep over the comparatively modest, if still extraordinary assertions of the Christian creeds—especially since they have an impressive pedigree in the two thousand years of Christian history.

The deeper question that troubles many thoughtful people is whether any form of worship, any plain statement of fact, any verbal conceptual statement of faith can be an adequate vehicle for expressing and sustaining the truths by which we seek to live. It is not only that we have learned to distrust words as an instrument of truth, even as a means of communication, but there seems to be a growing belief that religion is much more a matter of instinct than of thought. The words "I believe" then become a statement of my experience rather than of my convictions about God and what he has done, is doing, and will do in the world we know. This is why in theological circles there are signs of a retreat from the emphasis on the objective, the given, the revealed, and a return to Schleiermacher's definition of religion as "a feeling of absolute dependence." Rather than stand up and say: "I believe in God the Father Almighty" many would prefer some gesture of worship that means I acknowledge my total dependence on that God who is beyond me—and please don't ask me to define his nature.

It is not difficult to sympathize with this mood, especially if one has spent a lifetime in the business of verbalizing the Christian faith. What are the things a worshiper carries away from a church service? Not, normally, the words that were used to express our prayers, not the logic (if any) of the sermon, not even the words of Job or Paul at their most argumentative, and certainly not the words of the creeds. Much more likely it will be a moment when a baby was baptized, the total silence in which the bread and wine were received, or a vivid image from

Scripture or a sermon, or perhaps a phrase of music that evoked a sense of God's presence. It is increasingly the nonverbal, nonrational (not *irrational*), moments of worship through which, for many, God comes near, Christ becomes real, and the Holy Spirit moves. One might be tempted to say that this is good news for the Pentecostals and bad news for the Presbyterians were it not for other considerations to which I now turn.

You may have noticed that to convey this mood of turning away from words I have had to use words, and that in attempting to describe what happens beyond words I have used the concept of Father, Son, and Holy Spirit. It is impossible for beings with the gift of thought and the mysterious power of verbal communication to renounce these faculties in the name of some instinctive, entirely subjective, indescribable form of religion. Without accepting Descartes' famous dictum "I think: therefore I am," we are forced to recognize that for a mature human being there is no activity that can be totally abstracted from the reflection of the mind, no conviction that cannot, how ever inadequately, be put into words. What we call civilization is the product of this gift of thought and the possibility of the communication of ideas, and one of the greatest threats to the human race lies in the obliteration of the mind of the masses by the devices of propaganda, thought-control, and manipulation of the brain in the hands of a totalitarian power.

No one who has ever had an authentic religious experience can possibly believe that it is entirely translatable into words, and certainly not the plain prose of the historian, the journalist, or the scientist. When words are used as the language of faith they are apt to be deployed poetically as a symbol, image, and music to convey that which cannot be expressed otherwise. Some of the most powerful passages in the Bible are of this kind. When a scripture writer is describing his sense of God's call, his vision of the eternal, or such indescribable events as the creation or the end of the world, he does not use the language of a reporter, of a guidebook, or a lawyer's brief; he speaks of smoke and angels' wings, of clouds and trumpets and tongues of fire, of stars singing together and a voice "like the sound of many waters," of thunder and lightning and "a great white throne." It is only the prosaic, pragmatic modern Western mind that has been foolish enough to try to turn the bright language of biblical poetry into the prose of an insurance contract, and the dazzling imagery of apocalyptic into the factual information of an airline schedule (if you want to know what I am talking about, listen to the more lurid radio or TV evangelists running amok in the books of Daniel and Revelation). When I set out to make a case for the creeds I am not proposing that the Christian faith can be translated without remainder into plain statements of fact, or irrefutable logical propositions, or totally comprehensive concepts of the mind (I am reminded of the words about the Trinity in the Athanasian Creed: "The Father incomprehensible, the Son incomprehensible, and the Holy Ghost incomprehensible"—to which some wit added "and the *whole thing* incomprehensible").

Even when we admit that real religion cannot be expressed in verbal forms, and that the creeds themselves often use languge poetically and symbolically (in French the Apostles' Creed is called "La Symbole des Apôtres") we should not conclude that the Christian faith cannot be expressed in words, or cannot be grasped or communicated by the human mind. When I preached recently on the topic, What makes me a Christian? I obviously had some confidence in the possibility of communicating what this faith means to me even if the sermon was, I hope, something more than a series of propositions designed to persuade the mind. I could hardly have stood there in the pulpit and shrugged my shoulders.

So we find that the Christian church, from the beginning, sought to find ways to express what had happened when Jesus came, and died, and rose again. The Pentecost story shows in a fascinating way how the birth of the Church was also the birth of the creed. The second chapter of the book of Acts begins with a description of an experience of such religious intensity that it could not be described in the prose of a historian (even though some moderns would wish to describe it in the jargon of psychiatry). It is an experience of the Holy Spirit—which means that it is *both* supremely indescribable *and* recognizable to anyone who has ever known what it is to be moved to the depths by the presence of the Holy. In other words, we are in the presence of an event of such transcendence that it cannot be analyzed by the mind, yet of such reality that this is one of the few moments in which the history of the world was, in blunt fact, radically changed. The historian cannot tell us exactly what happened on that day, but he can most certainly trace the influence of this event on the group of people present who became the nucleus of the most powerful religious movement in the Western world. And, if he is not impervious to the dimension of the Spirit, he will be aware that this was only one manifestation, however cataclysmic, of the kind of religious illumination experienced by men and women from the dawn of history to the present day.

So we have, in the opening paragraph the Pentecost story, the language of symbol, the imagery of the transcendent—"the sound from heaven of a rushing, mighty wind," "the cloven tongues, like as of fire," "the filling with the Holy Ghost." Then, after what is described as "speaking with other tongues as the Spirit gave them utterance," Peter stood up and expressed the creed of the new community in plain words, "Ye men of Israel, hear these words; Jesus of Nazareth, a man approved of God among you by miracles and wonders and signs which God did by him in the midst of you, as ye yourselves also know: Him, being delivered by the determinate counsel and foreknowledge of God, ye have taken, and by wicked hands have crucified and slain: Whom God hath raised up, having loosed the pains of death: because it was not possible that he should be holden of it" (Acts 2:22-24). As recorded, this speech is the first confession of the Christian church, and you will notice that it underlines precisely what is said in the Apostles' Creed about Jesus Christ: his revelation of God, his crucifixion, his resurrection, his ascension to the right hand of God. Peter had clearly no inhibitions about putting into plain language the facts on which his own faith was based, nor did he hesitate to declare boldly and unmistakably to his compatriots the essence of his faith. "Therefore let all the house of Israel know assuredly, that God hath made this same Jesus, whom ye have crucified, both Lord and Christ" (Acts 2:36).

At first, of course, the infant Church used the language and idioms of their Jewish congregations. Peter's speech—his confession—may not have seemed to you altogether the kind of plain speech that we today would understand, but it was for his hearers. Later in the New Testament we find how these first Christians began to communicate the gospel to the Gentiles. Compare, for instance, Paul's way of talking about Jesus as the Messiah as he preached in the synagogues of the great cities, and the account of his declaration of his faith to the Areopagus in Athens. Then we have in the New Testament as a whole a vivid example of the translation of a Hebrew gospel into the common language of the Graeco-Roman world, the koine, as it was called, which was the lingua franca of the empire. Toward the end of John's Gospel we read, "These are written [and written in *Greek*] that ye might believe that Jesus is the Christ, the Son of God; and that believing ye might have life through his name." The first Christians clearly believed that their Good News could be expressed in words, whatever the language, and that faith could be awakened by their declaration and defense of what they believed.

In time it came about that certain words and phrases were so commonly used to confess the faith that they became, in effect, what we now know as creeds. The first Christian creed was probably *Kyrios Christos*—"Christ is Lord." This may have been the one confession of faith insisted on before baptism. It may seem a relatively simple creed, but these two words contain in embryo the doctrines that were later to be elaborated in the Apostles' and Nicene creeds, and were sufficient to make this new gospel what Paul called "a stumbling-block to the Jews and folly to the Greeks." This miniature creed made its witness clear enough and those two words were religious and political dynamite. For the word *Kyrios,* "Lord," was used of the Roman emperor as the supreme power to be venerated, and was also the word used for the most sacred name of God in the Greek translation of the Old Testament. *Christos* meant to the Gentiles who heard it simply the name of this Galilean whom the new Christian cult was worshiping, while for Jews it embodied a messianic claim.

The point is that these first Christians needed a form of worship in which to declare their faith, and there is other evidence in the New Testament of creeds which were probably used in services of worship. For instance, the form of words that Paul says he had received, probably at the time of his baptism, and had accepted as a member of the Church. "I handed on to you the facts which had been imparted to me: that Christ died for our sins, in accordance with the Scriptures; that he was buried; that he was raised to life on the third day, according to the Scriptures; and that he appeared to Cephas and afterwards to the twelve." In the First Epistle to Timothy we find these rhythmic lines which are almost certainly cited from a creed that was being used in worship:

> He who was manifested in the body,
> vindicated in the Spirit,
>   seen by angels,
> preached among the nations,
> believed on in the world,
>   taken up in glory. (3:16)

There are probably other early creeds in the New Testament records.

So, from the beginning, Christians found it not only possible but necessary to express their faith in a formula, a careful pattern of words which expressed what Luke called "those things which are most surely believed among us." It is striking that a young Gentile convert, dedicating his book to his patron Theophilus, indicated so clearly that he was not offering a collection of pious myths about a folk-hero called Jesus but was setting down the facts on which the specifically Christian beliefs were based. "Forasmuch as many have taken in hand to set forth in order a declaration of those things which are most surely believed among us, Even as they delivered them unto us, which from the beginning were eyewitnesses, and ministers of the word; It seemed good to me also, having had perfect understanding of all things from the very first, to write unto thee in order, most excellent Theophilus, That thou mightest know the certainty of those things, wherein thou hast been instructed" (Luke 1:1-4).

For a century or so it is probable that short creeds were used chiefly in worship where their constant repetition would remind the church members of central facts on which their faith was based and would serve to confess that faith to others. Such creeds might even be used when they were arrested and interrogated by the authorities. It was not until the second century that creeds more like those familiar to us came into being. They were used chiefly for the instruction of catechumens who would be required to assert them before baptism. Since baptism is in the name of the Father, the Son, and the Holy Spirit, these creeds, like the Nicene and the Apostles', had a trinitarian framework. It is this personal use of a creed that accounts for the words "I believe" in the preface to the creed we know. In our modern use it might be more helpful to say "We believe"—indicating that all are asserting the communal faith of the Church.

The more elaborate language of the Nicene Creed, let alone the Athanasian, was a later development. There was another factor that led the church to adopt these careful and succinct statements of the "the things most surely believed among us," the internal struggle with deviant views, chiefly concerning the person of Christ. Those with a taste for theological controversy could spend a lifetime digging into the various heresies, as they were called, that threw the church into turmoil as soon as it had ceased to be worried about persecution by the state and had settled in as the religious establishment of the Roman Empire. This is not the place for details about Arians, Sabellians, Nestorians, Monophysites, Donatists, and the various shades of gnosticism. Suffice it to say that most of the arguments centered on the divinity and humanity of Christ. The orthodox view that he is both truly divine and truly human was assailed from one side or the other until there was danger a Christ would emerge who was neither divine nor really human, but rather some kind of demigod. The historian Edward Gibbon licked his lips over the fury with which these questions were debated and spoke of the

Church's being split into factions violently warring over a dipthong. (For those who are interested, the dipthong in question is that which distinguished the Greek word *homoousios,* which means "of the same substance" and *homoiousios,* which means "of like substance." For Gibbon, and for most moderns, such a debate seems trivial. But for the serious Christian it does really matter whether Christ is really divine or simply "like the divine.")

It is always when the Church has relaxed its passion for evangelism and growth in Christ that internal debates break out, and the modern church, with its recent passion for what is called restructuring and for debating who may, or may not, be ordained, is in no position to cast stones at our ancestors who were engaged in the more serious business of theology. The real trouble in accepting and using today statements of faith, such as the assertion that Jesus was "of one substance with the Father," lies in the fact that fourth-century Christian thinkers were operating with philosophical categories which we no longer use. Not one worshiper in a thousand who repeats these words today could explain what is meant by "substance" or discourse on the Aristotelian distinction between "substance" and "accidents."

Then why should we use such creeds today? Chiefly because they are venerable and well-nigh universal testimonies to what, in essence, has been "most surely believed." That our belief in the divinity and humanity of Jesus is sometimes expressed in a language and philosophical framework unfamiliar to us, does not invalidate the magnificent assertion that "Christ is Lord." In the Apostles' Creed there is little that is totally obscure to a Christian today. I see such a creed as an anchor that is invaluable in a time of theological confusion such as ours, if we remember that it is not an idol to be worshiped or a legal definition of standard Christian belief to which we demand assent by every potential church member. The creed is an enduring link with Christians in every age and almost every land. We should be glad to lend our voices to this song of faith. (Incidentally, if we knew a little more about the ancient creeds and the controversies from which they came, we should not be surprised or upset over the appearance of books today that seem to challenge cherished beliefs and unsettle our deep convictions. I cannot think of any recent book of this kind that is not simply reopening a question that was much more thoroughly explored in the debates over the heresies of fifteen hundred years ago.)

Are we then to believe that the thinking of the Church froze so long ago and that we are bound to go on formulating our faith as our precursors did when these creeds were written? The subsequent history of the Church gives the answer. At the Reformation, for instance, there was an enormous theological upheaval as a result of which Calvinist and Lutheran churches, in particular, wrestled with new ways to confess the faith. The result was a flood of new confessions—Augsburg, Heidelberg, Scots, Westminster, to mention just a few. But none of the Reformers thought it necessary to renounce the Nicene or the Apostles' Creed. Presbyterians today, who feel that the introduction of the creeds into our worship represents an innovation or an aping of alien traditions, are usually surprised to learn that John Knox had the Apostles' Creed recited in every service he conducted.

And this wrestling and restating has continued into our own day. The German churchmen who resisted the neopaganism and idolatry of the Nazis were not theological radicals motivated by political or humanitarian concern, but, on the whole, orthodox Christians adhering to the doctrines of the historic creeds. At the Synod of Berman in 1934, however, they produced their own affirmation of the faith, their credo for the hour—which is one of the documents included, along with the Apostles' and Nicene creeds, in the *Book of Confessions of the United Presbyterian Church in the U.S.A.* There is no reason why the churches should not continue to think through the essence of the faith in each generation and try to express it in contemporary language. It is, however, a curious fact that the Apostles' Creed wears much better than any subsequent formulation. Occasionally I find in an old hymnbook some creed devised sixty or a hundred years ago, and it inevitably turns out to be more dated than those products of the great decisive age when the historic creeds came into being.

It is often said that, for the modern mind, the assertions of these creeds must be softened and the element of mystery eliminated from their majestic words. It is true that many genuine believers have difficulty in committing themselves to some phrases whose apparent meaning they either reject or do not understand. But it is remarkable that, in our generation, intellectuals of all kinds who have been converted to Christianity almost inevitably embrace or return to a vigorously orthodox form of the faith and are not at all attracted by the reductionist efforts of the more avant garde theologians. Listen to the novelist John Updike. "I call myself a Christian by defining 'a Christian' as a 'person willing to profess the Apostles' Creed.' I am willing, unlike most of my friends—many more moral than myself—to profess it (which does not mean understand it, or fill its every syllable with the breath of sainthood), because I know of no other combination of words that gives such life, that so seeks the crux. The creed asks us to believe not in Satan but only in the 'Hell' into which Christ descends. That Hell, in the sense at least of a profound and desolating absence, exists, I do not doubt; the newspapers give us its daily bulletins. And my sense of things, sentimental I fear, is that wherever a church spire is raised, though dismal slums surround it, and a single dazed widow kneels under it, this Hell is opposed by a rumor of good news, by an irrational confirmation of the plenitude we feel is our birthright."

I rest the case for the creeds.

4. "ALL THINGS ARE YOURS"
THE LEGACY OF CHRISTIAN HUMANISM

Those who would have us believe that the only live religious option for an inquiring citizen today is of the narrow, obscurantist, shrill variety are, of course, assuming that the churches that occupy the central ground of historical Christianity are moribund. They consider that the vast majority of professing Christians connected with these churches are either skeptics who feel that lip-service to faith is a small price to pay for maintaining an institution of great social value, the elderly who see in the Church a last bastion of the values by which they were raised, or the "neo-Confucians" whose religion consists in occasional visits to the shrines of their ancestors. The possibility of a live religion that is intelligent, humane, consistent with a full participation in contemporary culture, and yet basically orthodox, is dismissed out of hand. There is no such animal. To choose a religion, it is implied, is to choose some form of fanaticism. If one finds intellectual or cultural interests that do not fit into the dogmatic framework of the cult, then it is always possible to keep one's faith in a separate compartment. (You know how people sometimes whisper: "She's one of the most brilliant neurologists in the country—but did you know she is a Christian Scientist?" or "He's a very fine historian—but did you know he is a Mormon?")

So we have the current picture of the "true believer." True believers are regarded as being either the semi-educated and culturally deprived who are easy prey for any self-assured and sometimes unscrupulous evangelist, or the literate and cultured who manage to keep their religion in a discreet corner of the mind. One way or another religion is shunted onto the sidelines of modern society. This is indicated in popular speech by such expressions as "the church of your choice"—which implies that the worship and service of Almighty God is a matter of taste, like selecting a new tie or an automobile. One also hears people saying, by way of apology for daring to hold a certain belief: "I happen to be a Catholic"; "I happen to be a Seventh Day Adventist"; "I happen to be a Presbyterian." Religion then appears to be something that happens on the circumference of one's life, just as we say, "I happen to be left-handed," or "I happen to be allergic to oysters." You can hardly imagine Paul, in the presence of the Roman governor of Palestine, saying, "By the way, I happen to be a Christian."

Against this pressure to push religion into this category of the innocuous or fanatical stands this solid witness to a faith that will not go away—the faith that continues to say with the apostles, the fathers, the Reformers, and the inheritors of the civilization of the West: "I believe in God the Father Almighty . . . and in Jesus Christ his only Son our Lord . . . and in the Holy Ghost, the Lord and Giver of life." If, in spite of the ecumenical surge that is animating the credal churches and the fact that these churches still appeal to some of the most acute minds of our time, it is still asserted that the historic faith is moribund, the question arises What is to be put in its place? For, as Walter Lippman shrewdly observed fifty years ago, no such universal, widely accepted attitude to life has arisen to capture the thinking of the modern world, and to inspire its art. Fascism and communism, for instance, could now be described as much less influential than Christianity in the thought and culture of our day. Everyone recognized that fascism, with its grandiose and architecture, its vulgar paintings, its book-burnings, and its crippling of the creative spirit, was an impossible successor to Christianity as an animating ideology; but it is only recently that communion has been seen as following the same path, and Marxism as incapable of holding the allegiance of the free, inquiring spirit in either philosophy or science.) No great civilization, East or West, has ever appeared without some dominant set of beliefs about the human and the divine—about the nature of man and the power, or powers, that direct his course.

What has been surfacing as a possible ideology on which to base our human life and inspire our culture, is some form of what is called humanism. "Humanism," as will appear, is a tricky word which is claimed by a variety of philosophies from the atheist to the Christian. But increasingly it is being used with the accent on the *human* as opposed to the divine. The humanism that is being proposed today is known variously as "scientific humanism" (watch that adjective!—it always represents an attempt to enroll the prestige of modern science on behalf of some philosophy or religion), or, more accurately "rationalist humanism" (note the difference between rational, which we all try to be, and rationalist, which implies that there is no other avenue to truth than through our reason). The secular kind of humanism proposes that the basis for a truly civilized life should be the highest ideals that human beings have evolved over the centuries—individual freedom, tolerance, peace among the nations, and the constant battle against oppression, cruelty, ignorance, and disease. With such ideals, of course, the historic Christian church has no quarrel. The dividing line comes with the question of whether their ligitimacy and force come entirely from within the human family or whether they rest upon a divine foundation. The humanism that is offered as an alternative to any of the great religions of the world is radically atheistic.

This secular humanism has also produced its creeds. The last, as far as I know, was the Humanist Manifesto of 1973. It stated very clearly the fundamental difference between the humanism of the Christian tradition and what is now being offered in its place. A phrase which briefly hit the headlines at the time this manifesto came out stated: "No deity will save us; we must save ourselves." It went on to describe the religious faith that was being rejected: "We believe that traditional, dogmatic, or authoritarian religions that place revelation of God, ritual, or creed above human needs and experience do a disservice to the human species." To that it has to be replied that the historic Christian faith about which we have been talking in no sense confuses God, ritual, and creed. The faith of which I am speaking is based on the biblical proclamation of the sovereignty of God—"Thou shalt worship the Lord thy God, and him only thou shalt serve." In our review of the creeds a clear distinction surely emerges between the God whom we worship and the words which from time to time have been used to express who he is and what he has done. The Bible itself makes clear that ritual and creed are merely human attempts to express our dependence on him. But even to say that traditional religion places God above human needs and experience runs counter to the historic gospel that declares that God himself became man precisely in order to share our human needs and experience and to deliver us from our sins.

The religion attacked by this manifesto of secular humanism is not one that an orthodox Christian would recognize. It is the kind of entirely other-worldly faith that is to be found in deviant versions of Christianity and in many cults. This is what the Humanist Manifesto has to say: "Promises of immortal salvation, or fear of eternal damnation are both illusory and harmful. They distract humans from present concerns, from self-actualization, and from rectifying social injustices." This statement is so totally out of touch with both the Bible and the witness of the central stream of the faith that one hardly knows where to begin in taking it apart. Can anyone read Deuteronomy, Isaiah, or Amos and believe that the salvation they proclaimed had nothing to do with social justice? Can anyone examine the Gospels and come to the conclusion that Jesus was interested only in heavenly rewards and punishments, and said or did nothing about present human ailments, hunger, or oppression? And can any reasonable person ignore the enormous impact of the Christian church in the fields of education, health, justice, culture, and the alleviation of human distress? Secular humanists are entitled to reject religious beliefs as illusory, if that is their conviction, but they would have a difficult task in proving that the influence of the Hebrew prophets, of Jesus, of Francis of Assisi, of Erasmus, of Wesley, of Schweitzer, and of Bonhoeffer has been "harmful" and distracting "from present concerns."

Organized atheistic humanism of this kind is, curiously enough, numerically insignificant. The estimated number of adherents of organized humanism in this country is about 250,000, compared to church membership optimistically put at about 126 million. But it does represent the point of view of millions who have been convinced that traditional Christianity has become an impossible creed for our times and that our only hope lies in rescuing and reaffirming the best human ideals that have hitherto guided the destinies of the race. In the thinking of secular humanists it is assumed that there will be some kind of consensus as to what the good life really is. There is no criterion beyond what the manifesto called "human need and interest." And what is spelled out in that document looks remarkably like the typical program of the average progressive thinker or liberal politician.

"Humanism," as the word implies is a philosophy or way of life that puts an emphasis on human values, human aspirations, human achievements. It is thus distinguished not only from an outlook that concentrates on the realm of the divine, or supernatural, but also from that concerned chiefly with the world of nature. The word came into use at the time of the Renaissance when there was a "rebirth" of delight in the human concerns reflected in the art and literature of classical Greece and Rome. At that time humanism represented liberation from restrictions imposed on the creative spirit by the dogmas of the medieval church. Since then humanism has increasingly been seen as a protest against the kind of scientific point of view that ignores those human values that lie outside the normal investigation of science, or attempts to bring them under its control, (as do some modern schools of psychology) thus making all ethical judgments mere reflexes conditioned by our glands or our great-grandmothers.

Classical literature and art have a perennial appeal to all who delight in human values. Hence Latin and Greek appeared as "the Humanities" in the curricula of many universities, right to my own day in the University of Edinburgh. For centuries a thorough knowledge of Latin and Greek was regarded as the hallmark of a true education and of the cultured man or woman. (A certain cleric, preaching in Oxford about eighty years ago, ended with these oft-quoted words: "Nor can I do better, in conclusion, than impress upon you the study of Greek literature, which not only elevates above the vulgar herd, but leads not infrequently to positions of considerable emolument.") If he had lived to our day this gentleman would undoubtedly have exclaimed, *O tempora! O mores!* which one now has to translate: "Oh what times! Oh what habits."

Even though our times and our habits now seem as far removed from the influence of "the glory that was Greece and the grandeur that was Rome," as from that of the Greek and Hebrew scriptures, we cannot altogether wriggle out of our heritage. The ingredients of Western civilization have long been recognized as a combination of Greek culture, Roman law, and biblical inspiration, and a true modern humanism must take each of these into account. There will be those who would claim that the technological revolution that has swept upon us with such dizzying speed has totally outmoded any humanist philosophy that rests on such a heritage, but there are signs that not everyone is persuaded that modernity has freed the human spirit from its past. You will notice that when history has been ignored, nostalgia takes its place; and we are now flooded with popular sagas ranging from the Rome of "I, Claudius" to the high-jinks of the reign of King Edward VII. An informed humanism will always value the insights and achievements of the human spirit in all ages and recognize the peculiar contributions of the Hebrews, the Greeks, and the Romans.

The question now arises as to whether the religious strain in this mix is compatible with the humanism of the classics, or indeed with any true humanism at all. Many would argue that the biblical tradition with its emphasis on the sovereignty of God and the supremacy of what sounds like purely religious duties is the enemy of the free human spirit as expressed in the classics, the Renaissance, the Enlightenment, or in the culture of today. It will be asserted that the Bible not only contains prohibitions against the making of "graven images," and warnings against the seductive arts and graces of the pagan world, but is so other-worldly in its outlook that the good things of this life are despised in comparison with the blessings of heaven. Examples will be quoted of the hostility to the arts expressed by ancient iconoclasts, medieval prophets like Savonarola, the Puritans in England and America, and the dark suspicions of the Bible belt. How, it will be asked, can there be such a thing as Christian humanism when the Bible condemns the human race as sinful rebels against the holy God, and the record of the churches reveals such antagonism to human art and culture?

It has to be admitted that there has always been an ascetic strain in almost every religion that calls for a renunciation of many of the good things of this present world. There have been "saints" who rejected all human delights in order to concentrate on the vision of God. An early church father demanded to know what Jerusalem had to do with Athens, and a Puritan preacher once painted such a glowing picture of the superiority of the biblical story and religious ideas over the achivements of the human spirit that he announced: "An Aristotle was but the rubbish of an Adam, and Athens but the rudiment of Paradise." And to this day there is a vigorous strain of what Matthew Arnold called "Philistinism" in some evangelical circles where any devotion to the arts—whether the theater, painting, opera, or the dance—is frowned upon, and any study of secular philosophy or indulgence in the modern novel regarded as highly dangerous. It is thus part of the tactics of those who would ignore the mainstream of orthodox Christianity and present modern religion as an aberration of the human mind and spirit to suggest that belonging to a church is the equivalent of being banished to a ghetto of the culturally deprived.

It is not difficult to refute this lopsided estimate of the relationship of religion to the values of humanism, but it is not easy to get a hearing when there is such a clamor about the bigotry, obscurantism, and fanaticism of the true believer. Let me review some of the factors leading me to conclude that a Christian humanism not only is possible, but is a legacy of the Church which we must rediscover and present to the modern world as the truest humanism of all.

Let's begin with the Bible. In popular mythology the Bible is pictured as a purely religious book telling us about God and the supernatural world. It is, for instance, commonly thought that the Bible is chiefly concerned with telling us about heaven. Therefore it cannot possibly contribute to a humanism that values the good things of this present world. It comes as a surprise to many to be told that the Bible says very little about heaven, almost nothing in the Old Testament, and in the New just incidental remarks of Jesus and some florid imagery in the book of Revelation. On the other hand the Bible is packed with "human interest stories." Even a secular humanist who was prepared to brush aside all that is said about God would find the books of the Bible the richest mine in all literature for exploring the grandeur and the miseries of the human spirit. Every human situation, every human passion, every human longing, every human experience of joy and sorrow, every human aspiration for the good, the true, and the beautiful, is reflected in its pages. In the English-speaking world no other book has had such an influence on the greatest of its literary figures—Chaucer, Shakespeare, Milton, Johnson, Browning, and Tennyson, to name a few from the past, and on to Shaw, T. S. Eliot, and many contemporary poets, novelists, and dramatists. Whether believers or not, the greatest writers have reveled in the storehouse of character, narrative, and human drama between the covers of the Bible. It could indeed be argued that one of the counter-cultural, and counter-humanist forces in contemporary society has been the virtual disappearance from our schools and colleges of the King James Version of Scripture.

When we remember that the Old Testament is the foundation document of the Jewish people and consider for a moment the contribution of this people to the arts and humanities over the centuries, it will become even more apparent how absurd it is to think of the Bible as a basically antihumanist book. Our debt to the writers, the musicians, the scientists, the sculptors, and the great humanitarians of Jewish descent is so enormous that the Bible must rank as one of the most creative of all books for the human spirit.

When we turn to the New Testament and the origins of the Christian church, it has to be admitted that Jesus and his first followers were not greatly concerned with the art and culture of their day. Humanism, in the sense of proliferation of works of art, has normally required a relatively stable, and even comfortable, environment. The Jews of Jesus' time were not living in such a society, and there were few leisured people who could devote themselves to philosophy or art. We have to remember that the great humanists of classical times belonged to the minority who were supported in their style of life by a huge body of servants and slaves. And it was to the servants and slaves that Christianity made its first appeal. The humanism of Jesus was that of one who cared deeply about the welfare of the human beings around him whatever their position in society, and one who enjoyed the pleasures of human society to the extent that he was called a "glutton and a wine-bibber," and delighted in the beauty of the "lilies of the field." And the New Testament, like the Old, has comparatively little abstract teaching about religion, but a great many stories of intense human interest. The intense humanism of the parables has entered into the mainstream of the vocabulary and literature of the Western world.

The writers of the New Testament were, of course, not

concerned with producing works of art but with introducing men and women of all levels of education to the gospel of Christ. With the exception of Luke, and on occasion Paul, they did not write masterpieces of classical literature. They wrote in the Koine (the lingua franca of the Roman world), and their one purpose was to propagate the gospel and nourish the faith of the new Christians. Yet they inherited the Hebrew joy in creation and echoed the great humanist tradition of the Old Testament, including the famous question and answer of the psalmist: "When I consider thy heavens, the work of thy fingers, the moon and the stars which thou hast ordained, what is man, that thou art mindful of him? and the son of man that thou visitest him? For thou has made him a little lower than the angels and crowned him with glory and honor." That great declaration of religious humanism is matched by Paul's glorious hymn of love in I Corinthians 13. Was there ever a more moving and profoundly humanist utterance—from the very man who is so often accused of clamping grim religious doctrines on the spirit of man?

It was Paul who gave the lie to the accusation that Christianity is fundamentally an ascetic, world-renouncing creed when he wrote: "All things are yours and ye are Christ's, and Christ is God's." There is the great affirmation of Christian humanism. Notice how the historic creedal affirmation of Christianity, "Ye are Christ's, and Christ is God's," is linked to embracing and affirming all creation. "All things are yours," and elsewhere he defines "all things" in purely humanist terms. "Whatsoever things are true, whatsoever things are honest, whatsoever things are just, whatsoever things are lovely, whatsoever things are of good report . . . think on these things."

It may be true that the great apostle and his colleagues were so convinced that the crisis of the age had come with the death and resurrection of Christ, and so persuaded that

the final judgment was imminent, that they gave little, if
any, thought to the development of Christian philosophy,
Christian art, or a Christian civilization. Yet Paul, with his
education in the most erudite schools of Judaism, his
acquaintance with Greek poets, dramatists, and philosophers, and his cultured upbringing as a Roman citizen, could
well qualify for the title "humanist" as it was later
understood. What most certainly did happen as the Church
moved out into the mainstream of Graeco-Roman civilization was that it gradually won the respect of the pagan
world, not only for the quality of life reflected in its members,
but for its increasing ability to compete with the pagan world
in intellectual debate, and eventually for the quality of the
works of art that the faith inspired. And through the Dark
Ages it was the Church that preserved those humanist and
civilized qualities that were to burst out again at the time of
the Renaissance.

If it would be wrong-headed to attach the name
humanist to the majestic flowering of painting and
architecture in the Middle Ages, since it was the humanists
of the Renaissance who broke with the ecclesiastical
framework in which these works were produced, it would
still be narrow-minded to deny the creations of a Leonardo
da Vinci, a Michelangelo, or the builders of Chartres
Cathedral a place in the ranks of the loftiest expressions of
the human spirit in any age. And when we move on to
consider the art and literature inspired by the Reformation—the Rembrandts, the great composers of the seven-
teenth and eighteenth centuries, Milton and the metaphysi-
cal poets, Bunyan and the originators of the novel, not to
mention the scientific genius of a Newton—the expression
"Christian humanism" is surely abundantly justified.

If it should seem strange that a Presbyterian should
write with enthusiasm about humanism of any kind, let me
remind you that Calvin was one of the most noted humanist

scholars and an admirer of the arts. If the real model of the Christian humanist remains for us the attractive figure of Erasmus of Rotterdam, it still cannot be denied that both Luther and Calvin, by their classical training, their genius with words, their dialectical skill, and their appreciation of the sublime in all its forms, deserve the name humanist quite as much as the secularists and rationalists of our day.

"All things are yours." With these words the great apostle and evangelist invited the members of the Christian church to inherit the bounty and the beauty of this secular world in the name of Christ to whom they belonged, the Christ who himself uniquely belonged to God. The salvation that he proclaimed was not a purely mystical experience of union with Christ, not just an inward sense of release from sin and for heaven, and not only the realization of a new ethic by which to live. It carried with it also a new sense of what it means to be truly human and a new appreciation of the stories of creation, human and divine. "Behold, all things are become new." As the *shalom* of the Old Testament means much more than an absence of friction and war and suggests a human society permeated by the positive virtues of kindness, sensitivity, creativity, and love, so the salvation brought by Christ means much more than an escape from the hell of a meaningless, self-centered existence, and a promise of heaven. It has to do with the discovery here on this earth of all that reflects the goodness, truth, and beauty of the God who made us in the conviction that "the Spirit of men is the candle of the Lord."

Christian humanism, if you like, says "All this and heaven too"—if by heaven we mean the dimension of the eternal that surrounds us now as we trust the Father Almighty "Maker of heaven and earth" and that will be disclosed to us in the life everlasting.

To believe in Christ, to be a member of his Church, and to confess the historic faith is not to renounce and denounce the values and achievements of the human spirit, or even to regard them with a kind of grudging respect. It is to celebrate them as the gifts of the God on whom we all depend. The difference lies simply in our ultimate allegiance—the difference between shouting with Swinburne: "Glory to man in the highest, for man is the maker of things," and singing "Glory be to the Father, and to the Son, and to the Holy Spirit"—the Triune God who saw all that he had created, "and behold, it was very good."

"You never enjoy the world aright, till the sea itself floweth in your veins, till you are clothed with the heavens, and crowned with the stars; and perceive yourself to be the sole heir of the whole world, because men are in it who are everyone sole heirs as well as you. Till you can sing and rejoice and delight in God, as misers do in gold, and kings in sceptres, you never enjoy the world." So wrote the great Christian humanist Thomas Traherne.

5. *"AND GOD SAID . . ."*
REVISITING THE BIBLE

More than any book that was ever compiled the Bible has suffered from being talked about, written about, preached about, argued about, while not really being read. Therefore I hesitate to add another few thousand words about the Bible and—except for two things—would rather say: "Go away and read it." One is that being told to read it is another of those remarks about the Bible that keeps getting in our way; no one really wants to read a book that is always commended to us. The other is that, in spite of what we say about the Bible's being self-explanatory, we do need at least some guidance as to what kind of a book this is and where it came from.

Although the Bible continues to be the battleground for controversies about its meaning and its authority, there are some facts about it that are beyond dispute. It is, for instance, not a book but a collection of books composed over a period of several centuries. The Bibles we have are translations from the Hebrew and Greek of the original writers. None of the original manuscripts exist. What we have, as with any ancient book like Homer, Vergil, or Shakespeare, is the text established by the labors of scholars working on the vast number of copies that have been preserved. As in any other anthology of literature, the books in the Bible reflect the style, mannerisms, and cultural background of individual authors. I mention these obvious facts because of a lingering legend in some quarters that the Bible, in the King James Version, complete with black covers, dropped down from heaven shortly after the first Easter. It should also be mentioned, as beyond dispute, that no other collection of writings has had a greater influence on the religion, the ethics, the art, and the culture of the world.

It is also undeniable that the Bible has been, since very early days, the basic document, the literary lynchpin, of the Christian church. Whether it is claimed that the Bible created the Church or the Church the Bible (an argument that always reminds me of the chicken and the egg), there is no question at all as to the status of the Bible in matters of Christian belief and practice. To this day every church or cult that claims the name Christian makes its appeal, in one way or another, to the Bible. Even those that propagate doctrines totally at variance with the historic faith normally try to demonstrate that the Bible is on their side. "The Bible says . . ." is still regarded as the strongest weapon in any Christian controversy.

But this suggests another and rather disturbing fact about the Bible. If Christian people can cite its authority in support of contrary beliefs (for instance, the legitimacy of infant baptism), then it cannot be the kind of book that spells out in detail, and with legal precision, every item of Christian belief and tells us exactly what to do and what not to do in every conceivable circumstance. A glance at the Bible reveals at once that it is not such a book at all. While it contains a number of statements about God, about Christ, and about the Holy Spirit and has scattered through it certain specific directions (like the Ten Commandments and the Sermon on the Mount), the bulk of it consists of stories, songs, poetry, and sermons. In spite of all attempts to use the Bible as a ready reference book for doctrine, a timetable for future events, or an immediate settler of ethical arguments, it obstinately refuses to be such a book. A traveler opening a Gideon Bible in his hotel room may find pasted inside the cover some suggestions as to where to look if he is feeling depressed, or elated, or confused, but no one has yet been able to compile a biblical index which would show you where to find the answer to every religious or moral problem.

There is a dispute, of course, as to the literal authority any statement of the Bible must carry. But there can surely be no dispute about the fact that it is not set out like an encyclopedia or legal textbook. Nor can it be opened at random in the expectation that your theological or ethical question will be immediately answered. Suppose you wanted to know what God is like—and landed in the book of Esther where he is not mentioned at all; or, seeking guidance on the Christian attitude to war, found yourself in the middle of the book of Judges. It is fairly clear that even when the Bible is offering us specific instructions we have to take a lot of other factors into account.

There *is* a religious book that does claim this kind of encyclopedic and instant authority, and that is the Koran. It claims to have been dictated verbally by God and spells out Muslim beliefs and duties which are held to be inviolate and unaffected by the passage of time. We are watching now a concerted effort to create Islamic states for which the commands of the Koran would be binding. There have been, of course, so-called "Christian states", but even in Calvin's Geneva, with its intensely biblical theology, there was no attempt to use the Bible as a legal code book. No one honored the Scriptures more than Luther and Calvin, but neither of them allowed the Bible to become the direct and immediate representative of God himself. For them the final Word was not a book but Christ himself. Luther could even speak scathingly of a book like the Epistle of James, which he felt did not sufficiently proclaim the gospel of salvation by faith in Christ, while Calvin always insisted that to understand the Bible we need more than the literal words; we must have the "interior witness of the Holy Spirit."

Yet in our day there is a surprisingly powerful trend in evangelical circles to claim for the Bible the kind of infallibility that Islam claims for the Koran. In reaction to the neglect of the Bible in the mainline churches and the consequent loss of zeal for evangelism, there has been a revival of the idea of the "infallibility," and "inerrancy" of the Scriptures. Both words, of course, need definition. Until recently ministers and elders in the United Presbyterian Church were required to answer the question: "Do you believe the Scriptures of the Old and New Testaments to be the Word of God, the only infallible rule of faith and practice?" By answering yes most candidates probably meant that the Bible is our unique authority and guide which will not lead us astray in matters of faith and practice. "Inerrancy" can also be understood in the sense that it is the one reliable document for establishing what we are to believe and how we are to live. But both words have, for most people, a stronger meaning, and inerrancy is often now proclaimed as indicating that the Bible cannot possibly contain any statement that is inaccurate, whether in the realm of theology, history, science, or any other.

While having the utmost respect for many devoted and zealous Christians who hold this view, I believe it to be not only untenable but a distortion of the witness of the Bible itself and damaging to the Christian cause. It can be held only by an exercise of mental gymnastics no Christian should be required to make and by indulging in sophistry unworthy of our faith. If, for instance, two divergent accounts of a certain incident occur in the historical sections of the Old Testament, every conceivable and inconceivable argument is produced to reconcile them, instead of a sober acceptance of the Bible's testimony to the fact that the two writers either had access to different sources, or held different views as to their significance. If John's Gospel puts the cleansing of the temple at the beginning of Jesus' ministry and the Synoptic Gospels put it at the end instead of admitting that the writers were operating with a different framework of time, the inerrancy school is forced to maintain that the same incident occurred twice. If one account says that three people were with Jesus and another says two, then the argument is used that three includes two. If, finally, two totally different numbers are given, one in Kings and one in Chronicles, there is the unfailing last resort—in the original manuscript the numbers were the same!

When it comes to the ethical difficulties of this view, it soon becomes plain that even the most rigid adherent of inerrancy has his own way of skimming over the problem. When the psalmist curses the city of Babylon with the words, "Happy shall be he, that taketh thy little ones and dasheth them against the stones," he may fall back on the argument that, although this is not an infallible revelation of the will of God, it is an inerrant transcription of the state of mind of the psalmist! When an older friend of mine for whom I had a great respect once complained to me that ministers of our church today were not taking the Bible literally, I asked him what he would do with the plain injunction, "Thou shalt not suffer a witch to live." He just muttered something about that being an exception.

Not only are such mental acrobatics totally unnecessary if we accept the Bible as it is, but the total inerrancy doctrine can lead to serious consequences for the life of faith. Suppose a youngster who has had this doctrine instilled in him comes across the words of Jesus about the mustard seed—"the least of all seeds" he says—and then discovers from his botany class that there are many seeds smaller than the mustard. "Oh dear," he says to himself, "a mistake—then the Bible isn't inerrant. Therefore I can't trust anything it says, not even when Jesus is speaking."

Few people, one hopes, will be victims of this kind of reasoning, but casualties of a too-rigid view of scriptural inspiration are to be found among our friends and acquaintances. Among the older generation today, there are many who did not entirely abandon the Church when they discovered that there could be mistakes in the Bible, but settled for a view of the Bible as an interesting collection of ancient religious literature which they wished preachers would not go on calling the Word of God. Once the battle for the acceptance of historical and literary critical methods as applied to the Bible was won in the seminaries of the major denominations, there was an inevitable reaction. Biblical scholars, especially the Germans with their passion for the pursuit of a theory, began to deny the historicity, not only of Adam and Eve, but of the patriarchs, of Moses, of the apostles, and finally queried even the actual existence of Jesus himself. The Church entered a period of theological liberalism when the Bible lost its authority and became merely a quarry from which to extract those ideas that fitted in with the humanitarian sentiment, political idealism, and evolutionary optimism of the time.

Thus we seem again to be up against the dilemma of skepticism and fanticism. Many seem to feel that the only alternative to a blind adherence to an inerrant Bible is a skepticism that cannot admit that the content of these ancient books can be in any genuine way a Word of God for us today (I was once asked point-blank after a service how I could possibly follow the savage story of David riding back to Jerusalem in triumph with the bloody head of Goliath with the words, "The Lord bless to us the reading of his holy

Word"). For those of us who believe that the future of the Church lies with the solid body of Christians who are neither skeptics nor fanatics but adhere to the central doctrines of the faith, the question is how to deal with the Bible; or, rather, how to let the Bible deal with us. How do we accept the results of a sound and balanced critical analysis of the biblical documents and at the same time hear the Word of God that is the basis of our faith?

It would not, of course, be fair to label all who hold to the inerrancy doctrine of the Bible as fanatics, but one of the factors that bedevils us today is the use of the Bible by what is unkindly referred to as the lunatic fringe of modern evangelism. The wild-eyed, self-assured propagator of his own brand of religion usually has a Bible at his fingertips from which he extracts the texts he needs to make his case (which may have little to do with the historic Christian faith). He is the infallible interpreter of Scripture, just as his rival on another network equally claims to be (incidentally, we learn from this the lesson that a really infallible Bible demands a really infallible interpreter, which is another reason for rejecting any theory of inerrancy).

How then are we to read the Bible in our homes, hear it in our churches, and use it as our authority for faith and practice?

First, we should recognize that the apparent paradox of hearing God addressing us through truly human writings, composed and edited like any other book, is not unique in our Christian experience. In fact, it parallels almost exactly the foundation doctrine of the faith—the Incarnation, the belief that God himself became man in Jesus Christ. "Who for us men, and for our salvation" says the Nicene Creed, "came down from heaven; and was incarnate by the Holy Ghost of the Virgin Mary, *and was made man.*" The faith that is still here proclaims not only the divinity of Jesus Christ but his complete humanity. He was no apparition, or demigod, but one like us. It is through his oneness with us in our humanity that he brings us to the living God. Similarly we can say that the Bible is no magic book, not even strictly speaking a *religious* book, but a totally human book through which we hear the Word of God himself. The doctrine of the Incarnation is thus reflected in our understanding of the Bible, just as it is in the Sacrament of the Lord's Supper. The bread and the wine are not magical elements, or even "holy" materials to be obtained from a religious store, but the ordinary common things that are in daily use. And yet with their reception we are united with Christ himself. A sacramental view of the Bible means a belief that, by the power of the Holy Spirit, these very human documents can convey to us nothing less than a Word of God.

It is time to say something more about the meaning of such expressions in the Bible as, "The Word of the Lord came to me" or "And God said" or "Thus saith the Lord." What is really meant? Liberal theology has tended to offer the quick answer that this was merely the contemporary way for the writer to say, "I have an overwhelming impression that this is the message God wants me to proclaim." It is probably true that the prophets who used these expressions did not expect to be understood as saying they actually heard a voice from heaven dictating what they were to write. They did not expect their books to be read by prosaic, literal-minded Westerners, unaccustomed to the symbolic language of the Semitic peoples. Yet we have to be wary about the dogmatism of the so-called modern mind. Recent discoveries indicate that a certain portion of the brain may have direct access to the realm of the spirit, and in view of this we should be cautious about reducing all scriptural statements about hearing the Word of God to a rational process of reflection. However, leaving room, as we surely must, for the element of mystery in such prophetic writing, clearly "Word of God" is a metaphor.

How do I use a word? What happens when I stand up before a group of people and give utterance? First, it is my fond belief that at least something of the thoughts that are in my mind will be conveyed to other minds. In the same way, the Word of God is a conveying of his thoughts to us. But something more is happening every time I speak. I am, in a very real sense, giving myself to you. It is thus true that every time we speak we are giving ourselves away. And that is what the Bible claims is happening through what it calls the Word of God.

The prologue to John's Gospel opens with the astonishing words that echo the beginning of Genesis, "In the beginning . . . was the Word." The God of Genesis who "made the heaven and the earth" did so because he is a living God, a God who expresses himself, thus a God who speaks. "And God said . . . and God said . . . and God said . . . ," and the universe in all its diversity came into being. The rest of the Bible tells us that he is still speaking, still revealing himself, still giving himself away. Later in that prologue come the climactic verse: "And the Word was made flesh and dwelt among us." The self-giving of God of which the whole Old Testament speaks is a preparation for this stupendous self-giving which is the coming of Christ. He is *the* Word of God, and it is in the light of his incarnation that all the rest of the biblical revelation is to be seen and understood.

The writer of the Epistle to the Hebrews opens his book with a similar statement using a different image. "When in former times God spoke to our forefathers, he spoke in fragmentary and varied fashion through the prophets. But in this final age he has spoken to us in the Son whom he has made heir to the whole universe." Again there is the note of finality with the coming of Christ. The testimony of the Old Testament writers is "fragmentary and varied." The supreme Word of God is spoken in his Son—the perfect reflection of God's being and his love.

The Roman Catholic, Protestant, and Anglican churches are on the whole united today in this understanding of the Scriptures. Within these denominations there is still some divergence as to the nature of scriptural inspiration, but there is a growing convergence on the nature and use of the Bible. In recent years there has been a remarkable sharing in biblical scholarship, new translations of the Bible, and its use both in theology and the devotion of Christian people. The United Presbyterian Church in the U.S.A. in its *Confession of 1967* makes the following statement which, I believe, would win general acceptance in that great body of Christians who profess the historic faith:

The one sufficient revelation of God is Jesus Christ, the Word of God incarnate, to whom the Holy Spirit bears unique and authoritative witness through the Holy Scriptures, which are received and obeyed as the word of God written. The Scriptures are not a witness among others, but the witness without parallel. The church has received the books of the Old and New Testaments as prophetic and apostolic testimony in which it hears the word of God and by which its faith and obedience are nourished and regulated.

The New Testament is the recorded testimony of apostles to the coming of the Messiah, Jesus of Nazareth, and the sending of the Holy Spirit to the Church. The Old Testament bears witness to God's faithfulness in his covenant with Israel and points the way to the fulfillment of his purpose in Christ. The Old Testament is indispensable to understanding the New, and is not itself fully understood without the New.

The Bible is to be interpreted in the light of its witness to God's work of reconciliation in Christ. The Scriptures, given under the guidance of the Holy Spirit, are nevertheless the words of men, conditioned by the language, thought-forms, and literary fashions of the places and times at which they were written. They reflect views of life, history, and the cosmos which were then current. The church, therefore, has an obligation to approach the Scriptures with literary and historical understanding. As God has spoken his word in diverse cultural situations, the church is confident that he will continue to speak through the Scriptures in a changing world and in every form of human culture.

God's word is spoken to his church today where Scriptures are faithfully preached and attentively read in dependence on the illumination of the Holy Spirit and with readiness to receive their truth and direction.

If we revisit the Bible with such an understanding of its nature, we shall be delivered from the dilemma of having either to defend the historic and scientific accuracy of every statement and the morality of every tale or having to regard it as ancient literature with no more claim on our attention than Plato, Shakespeare, or Pascal. We should try to let the Bible speak for itself, which is an extremely difficult thing to do, since most of us have been conditioned to approach it with the adjective "holy" getting in our way or as a quarry for proof texts in support of certain doctrines or skeptically as a collection of fairytales of doubtful value or devotionally as a collection of isolated verses for our edification and comfort. We have all had to struggle with the legacy of confusion left us by the habit of hearing snippets of the Bible read in church and need to give these books a chance to make their impression as a whole. We would also profit by asking ourselves if there is any kind of unity or development to be discovered to link the various sections of the Bible.

My impression is that exposure to these books as they stand will lead to the conclusion that they represent an ongoing conversation between God and man—a conversation into which we find ourselves drawn. And without question that conversation comes to a glaring focus in the Gospels where we are introduced to the Word made flesh in Jesus Christ. The strange power which we have experienced in these books (or, if we ourselves haven't, we know millions of people have experienced it in every age) is the work of the Holy Spirit who alone, as Calvin clearly said, is able to "open our eyes to the truth that lies in this extraordinary collection of books."

What is needed, if the historic faith is to spring to life in this central block of Christians of whom I have been speaking, is a fresh, serious, and even passionate study of the Bible, worship, and preaching that are centered on it as they have not always been in recent years, and a readiness to translate its message in terms our contemporaries can understand and in specific acts of obedience, individually and socially, to this Word of God.

"God hath yet more light."

6. "LET US WORSHIP GOD"
WHY? HOW? WHEN? WHERE?

On any Sunday morning about 40 percent of the population of the United States attends church, presumably for the worship of God. According to the Gallup polls, that has been roughly the figure for the last ten years, showing a decline from a staggering 50 percent in 1955.

I find the figure 40 percent staggering enough. The skeptic in me is apt to spring to life at the sound of a public poll. If every other person in Manhattan went to church on a given Sunday, there simply would not be enough room to receive them. However, as we know, Manhattan is not America, and there is no doubt that far more people attend worship across this country than in any other part of the world.

The bulk of this worshiping community belongs to that central mass of believing Christians who are neither skeptics nor fanatics but hold to what we have been calling the historic faith. Skeptics either do not go to church at all, or ally themselves with creedless denominations, or maintain a Christmas/Easter relationship with the church of their fathers. The more fanatical sects, especially those that have gained a radio and TV following, are not really concerned with what the Church has known as the public worship of God. In fact, they may well have contributed to its decline, as thousands have convinced themselves that they have fulfilled their religious duties by lapping up what is offered on the little screen.

So it is the traditional churches, by and large, that maintain on an impressive scale this heritage of gathering together for common worship. This phenomenon is not newsworthy; it is simply accepted as a familiar facet of American life. Only when a service is disrupted by some agitator or when a preacher makes a sensational pronouncement on some controversial topic, would the media be likely to pay any attention. Yet, if that legendary visitor from Mars were to visit this corner of our planet, he would surely be struck by the fact that such a large proportion of the population flocks into these curious buildings once a week to engage in a great variety of exercises centering on a God whom no one has ever seen.

That thought leads us straight to the questions: What is worship and why should anyone want to share in it?

The dictionary defines worship as "(1) reverent honor and homage paid to God, or a sacred personage, or to any object regarded as sacred; (2) formal or ceremonial rendering of such honor and homage." That definition covers all kinds of religious worship including what we call idolatry. We are not concerned with the metaphorical use of the word to denote as excessive love of money, possessions, or the object of one's affections.

It is this primary definition of worship as "reverent honor and homage paid to God" that should rule our thinking about what goes on in the churches every Sunday morning. We have to confess that in recent years this simple truth has been obscured by all kinds of different notions about the meaning of church services. For some this coming together is a social occasion with a religious flavor. For others, particularly in Protestantism, it is a regular opportunity to be spiritually stirred or nourished by a sermon (hence the common remark, "I'm going to hear Dr. So-and-so," instead of "I'm going to worship God.") Many today think of worship as a mild form of therapy for the mind and soul. Others think of it as an enriching aesthetic experience, while even more see it as a religious Rotary, a getting together with like-minded people to stimulate service to the community. One way or another, there has been in recent decades a secularization of divine worship. The emphasis has been on the horizontal plane of its social, psychological, and educational benefits rather than on that vertical dimension of response to God which is the one quality that distinguishes it from every other human activity. The *Book of Order of the United Presbyterian Church in the U.S.A.* opens the chapter on the worship of God with the blunt reminder: "In worship the initiative lies with God, as it does in all of his dealings with people."

The answer to the question Why worship? then depends entirely on our answer to the other question: Do you believe in God? If anyone answers in the negative I can think of no reason whatever why they should be expected to come to a service of worship, unless through sheer curiosity, nostaligia, or a wistful hope. But if the answer is yes—and once again the polls produce a mind-boggling 94 percent who say they believe in God and an even more astonishing 80 percent who profess to believe that Jesus is his Son—then surely there can be no question about the obligation to give him "reverent honor and homage." We may argue about the precise methods of so doing, and we shall have to deal with the how and the when and the where, but there is no logical way we can profess to believe in God Almighty and at the same time reject any notion of acknowledging him in worship. Really to believe in God, the "maker of heaven and earth" on whom we depend from day to day *must* mean offering him our reverence, devotion, and praise. The first words Jesus has taught us to say are not a petition, confession, or an intercession, but sheer worship. "Our Father who art in heaven, *hallowed be thy name.*" Today these may well be the least understood words in the entire prayer.

What makes this call to worship difficult for many of us is our diminished sense of the holy. A greater proportion of Americans may profess to believe in God than when this nation was founded, but that sense of awe, of mystery, of the numinous is far less common today. For a while it was not encouraged in many Protestant churches. Rather every effort was made to eliminate from the language, the ritual, the architecture, and the furnishing, anything that was not plain and clear and eminently sensible. The tragedy is that, by leaning toward the skeptic by rubbing out whatever had a supernatural flavor, such churches drove a generation that was seeking the transcendent into the arms of the cults. The liturgical revisers who removed the angels and archangels from the great Communion prayer helped to rob the Sanctus ("Holy, holy, holy, Lord God of hosts") of its overtones of mystery and wonder. If the central body of Christians who profess the historic faith are to demonstrate the power of the Spirit in this generation, we need to recover this note of profound and adoring worship.

A practical difficulty that gets in the way of many who are trying to understand what worship really means is the nagging thought that surely God is not a kind of oriental potentate who has an insatiable appetite for flattery and praise. Is God really a being who needs to be constantly told "How great thou art!" whenever his children gather to address him? Why do the psalms keep insisting that we praise the name of the Lord and remind him of his power and glory? What is this adoration that is implied by the word "worship"?

We will understand it much better if we forget about the oriental despot and concentrate instead on the spontaneous expressions of gratitude and wonder that spring from our hearts whenever we experience what is supremely worthy of our praise and admiration—a glorious passage of music, a thrilling production of "Hamlet," an unforgettable sunset, a beautiful act of generosity, or even, if you like, a magnificent rally in a tennis tournament. Our hallelujahs are akin to our bravos; the outpouring of delight in that which is both beyond us and yet unbelievably satisfying and enriching. Only those who are incapable of such response could be said to exclude themselves from the true experience of worship. Adoration is not concocting extravaganzas of flattery to present to a demanding God. It is much more like that whispered "how wonderful!" with which we share with one we love the richest experiences that life has to offer.

The deeper our belief in God, then, the more certain it is that we shall want to offer this "reverence, honor, and homage." But now come the questions of the How? When? and Where?

We can well imagine someone thoroughly agreeing that the worship of God is our duty and delight, but raising at once the question as to why it must happen with a motley group of people in a specially constructed building at eleven o'clock on Sunday morning. One of the most salient features of the current surge toward religion is the assertion of an individual faith and the rejection of all that smacks of organized religion. A recent investigation into the convictions of both church members and the unchurched yielded some startling figures. To the proposition "An individual should arrive at his or her own religious beliefs independent of any churches or synagogues," 65 percent of the unchurched, not surprisingly, said yes. What is astonishing is that 51 percent of the church members agreed. It is reasonable to conclude that more than half of those who do attend worship, at least occasionally, are convinced that they can very well do without it. This is such a powerful trend that it must have a lot to do with the lack of a strong and attractive witness of worship on the part of the great central body of church people whose "faith is still there." Once again there has been a failure of leadership in the thinking through and the teaching of our Christian heritage.

The question at issue here is that of *public* worship. It is, of course, perfectly true that anyone can, and should, worship alone at any time and in any place. But there has been no world religion, least of all Christianity, that has ignored or dispensed with communal worship. The Old Testament offers abundant examples of what could be called private worship, but its major emphasis is on the coming together of the people of God to serve and praise him. Whole sections of the literature of the Psalms are devoted to descriptions of the public worship of the Lord and instructions as to how it should be done. We should note too how many of these psalms reflect the worship of the Temple, and were, in fact, hymns to be chanted by these congregations. There used to be a theory that the prophets were sturdy individualists who rejected the ritual of the Temple and called for an individual worship expressed in Micah's words: "What doth the Lord require of *thee*, but to do justly, and to love mercy, and to walk humbly with *thy* God?" The priests were thus caricatured as the upholders and beneficiaries of the public ritual which was grossly unspiritual and corrupt. Few scholars would now accept this description of the prophets. After all, it was in the temple at Jerusalem, probably in the middle of a highly complicated ritual, that the young Isaiah had his vision and his call. The first concern of men like Ezra and Nehemiah, after the return from exile, was to rebuild the temple and reconstruct the inherited ritual. The prophets were not destroyers but reformers of the public worship of God. We cannot understand the Old Testament unless we realize the pervasive sense of the community of the people who are called together to worship and to serve the Lord.

The evidence in the New Testament concerning the worship forms of the first Christians is not copious and certainly offers little to denominational enthusiasts who like to claim that their form of worship is infallibly prescribed by the apostles. But there is no doubt whatever about the fact that Christianity was from the beginning expressed in a community called the Church and that common worship was a major part of its life. The Church was born in a dazzling moment of communal praise and adoration when the Holy Spirit came upon the disciples at Pentecost, and without this constant assembling for worship through the centuries Christianity would never have survived.

We find, however, that from the beginning there were always some Christians who felt they could do without communal worship. The apostles saw in these assemblies for worship an indispensable stimulus for giving glory to God and strengthening one another in the faith, but one of them, writing to Christians in Rome, incidentally reveals that skipping church is a practice with a long history. "We ought to see," he writes, "how each of us may best arouse others to love and active goodness, *not staying away from our meetings, as some do,* but rather encouraging one another." With these words the apostle puts his finger on one weakness in the argument that one can worship God and be a true Christian without sharing in the coming-together at a specific place. To withdraw from, or to neglect, the "assembling together" of which the New Testament speaks so often, is to be deprived of the natural encouragement and support that is so real a part of the Christian life—what we call the communion of the saints, or the fellowship of the Holy Spirit. It is remarkable how, when Christians suffer any kind of persecution, the coming together for worship is always seen as being of vital importance. From the catacombs of ancient Rome to the underground churches in many parts of the world today, Christians have risked their lives for the sake of their common worship.

Another factor sometimes overlooked by the Christian individualist who claims the right to worship where and how and when seems best to him or her is that of discipline—a word which, we are apt to forget, is cognate with "discipleship." The blunt fact is that, without some discipline of coming together at a certain time in a certain place, to worship God, to commune with the risen Christ, and to seek the empowering of the Spirit, we are apt to let our daily round crowd such thoughts from our minds. Every minister is familiar with the remark, "I can worship God on the golf course as well as in church." And every minister is tempted to reply, "Of course, but *do* you?"

But the ultimate answer to this Christian individualism, this strong desire for a religion untrammelled by churches, worship services, sacraments, and clergy, is that it is based on a fallacy. Ask anyone who claims to have thought out his own religion and to be free from any obligation to join in the life and worship of a church just what, in fact, he believes. Almost every time they will spell out doctrines that they inherited from the witness of the Church Catholic (I am using that shorthand phrase to describe the central body of Christians who hold the historic faith). They did not pluck out of the air the belief that God is love, that we ought to love him and our neighbor, that the Spirit of God is everywhere inspiring us to a generous and unselfish life. All these teachings were received, at first, second, or third hand, from the Christian church, and it is highly unlikely that an individual would have thought of any of them if he had been born on a cannibal island a hundred years ago. It is the worshiping community, known as the Body of Christ on earth, that has under God professed these beliefs and instilled them into every society where it has taken root. If the so-called organized religion of the churches had not existed, very few of the convictions of the modern religious individualist would have ever occurred to him.

It is especially remarkable that even the more astonishing and unprecedented doctrines of the Christian faith are professed by those who claim a religion totally independent of the churches. Consider these two findings of the Gallup poll. We have seen that 65 percent of the unchurched believe that an individual should arrive at his or her own religious beliefs independent of any churches. Yet, according to the same poll nearly the same percentage of the unchurched (64 percent) claim to believe that Jesus Christ is God. Who told them?

What seems to block so many from participation in the worship of the Church Catholic is not a discovery that religion is something that they can acquire and develop satisfactorily on their own, but the nature of the worship in many of the churches within their reach. Too often it appears lifeless, stereotyped, and remote from life as they know it. And here we come up against the century-old problem of how the inevitable forms and rituals of public worship can be consonant with Jesus' call to worship the Father in spirit and in truth. Our dictionary, you remember, defined worship as (1) reverent honor and homage paid to God; and (2) formal or ceremonious rendering of such honor and homage. The distinction here is not between a true worship, which is, as it were, entirely spiritual, and the corruptions that ensue whenever we try to formalize it. Rather it is the distinction between the love that a man may steadily have for his wife, and the little ceremonies and gifts by which he expresses it. I doubt if many wives would be satisfied with an assurance of love that was never expressed in physical ways or in birthday or anniversary gifts.

The Church Catholic has from its beginning used forms and ceremonies to express the adoration and dedication that the gospel elicits from the believer. The word "ritual" is offensive only to those who imagine that their favorite style of worship involves no order of any kind—which is impossible. No community can meet for any purpose whatever without evolving a ritual. The question is simply whether a ritual becomes an end in itself or is always devised and used as a means of worshiping in spirit and in truth. We have noted how the prophets denounced a temple ritual that had become not only sterile but a substitute for genuine obedience to God's commands. This is why Amos put these sarcastic words in the mouth of God: "I hate, I spurn your pilgrim-feasts; I will not delight in your sacred ceremonies. When you present your sacrifices and offerings I will not accept them, nor look on the buffaloes of your shared-offerings. Spare me the sound of your songs; I cannot endure the music of your lutes. Let justice roll like a river and righteousness like an ever-flowing stream."

In the same way the Christian church time and again has had to listen to that same prophetic voice denouncing worship that has become an empty ritual, a barrier between the people and the gospel of Christ. Not only during the Reformation, but regularly since then, worship has had to be revised and revitalized and made a more adequate instrument for the adoration of the Almighty, the hearing of the gospel, and the call to discipleship.

During the last twenty years there has been a considerable upheaval in the worship of the denominations that comprise this church Catholic in our country and abroad. Under the name of liturgical renewal there have been great changes, particularly in the Roman Catholic and Anglican communions, such as the replacing of the altar with the Communion table, the use of the vernacular, and the introduction of new hymns and modes of music. Other churches have felt the impact, and there have been lively controversies about what some call bringing worship up to date and alive, and others call needless tampering with beloved forms of words and treasured ways of worship. Two things have to be kept in mind. (1) There cannot be a static form of worship that will remain valid and helpful to the end of time. It is hard for some to realize that there was a first time when the Nicene Creed was used, a first time when Latin prayers were translated into English, a first time when the King James Version was read in church—even a first time when a congregation heard "Rock of Ages" —and probably grumbled about "unknown hymns." (2) On the other hand, we should keep in mind that worship, of all human activities, is one in which settled and accepted forms should not be constantly and thoughtlessly tampered with. (C. S. Lewis said somewhere that he, as a layman, did not really care what order his rector used so long as he didn't change it.) Most people find it easier to worship if they are not wondering what is going to happen next.

Let me conclude by summarizing what I feel to be needed if this church Catholic is going to declare boldy and, I hope, beautifully that "the faith is still there!"

There must be a renewal of the sense of the holy. That comes before any attempt to design worship that appeals to our secular society. In word and sacrament it must be made plain that we are inviting all to worship the transcendent God and are responding to a supernatural gospel.

At the same time worship must be truly human, expressing contemporary needs, and avoiding peculiarly "religious" language or a "churchy" atmosphere.

Worship must express more than is customary the warmth of a truly Christian family where we do indeed "arouse each other to love and active goodness."

And that last phrase reminds us that living worship cannot stop at the church door. If the church Catholic is to have the impact that we pray for, its worship must spill over from the sanctuary to an "active goodness" that works for the realization of those things for which we have prayed.